"I enthusiastically recommend this book to anyone facing the difficult invitation of grief's embrace.

"*Grief Is a Dancer* is at once both heartbreaking and inspiring. Its pages are engaging and filled with precious invitations to hope and healing.

"The confessions, tears, and even moments of sweet laughter that its stories evoke are restorative.

"Alisa's book is a message of hope that's meant to be shared—offered gently, graciously, by one who has been there."

—DAVID E. WOOLVERTON, SENIOR PASTOR,
ST. PAUL'S CHURCH, ELIZABETHTOWN, PA

GRIEF
IS A
DANCER

A MEMOIR

A mother reflects on the rigor and beauty
of grief, 25 years after losing her child

Alisa Bair

WALNUT
STREET
BOOKS

LANCASTER,
PENNSYLVANIA

walnutstreetbooks.com

Cover and page design by Cliff Snyder

Grief Is a Dancer
Copyright © 2021 by Alisa Bair

Photo by Sergey Nivens: front and back covers.
Photos by author: dedication page. Photo by Linda Metz: page 231.
Photo by Red Accordion Studios Photography: page 240.

Paperback: 9781947597402
PDF: 9781947597419
EPUB: 9781947597419
Kindle: 9781947597419

Library of Congress Control Number: Data available.

Grief Is a Dancer is published by
Walnut Street Books, Lancaster, Pennsylvania

info@walnutstreetbooks.com

To my husband Rob,
and to the beautiful, brilliant lights of our lives,
Lauren, Leslie,

and Kelly
(1985—1993)

Contents

Necessary grief when shunned or unattended can easily hide for years, even generations, in the skeletal structure of the family collective psyche...

So, best to grieve when it's time, to save the world a lot of war and trouble.

—MARTÍN PRECHTEL

CHAPTER ONE

Twenty-Five Septembers

September 20, 2018

It is an overcast Thursday, temps in the low 70s. My husband, Rob, returns home late from work and picks me up so we can get to the cemetery before dark. We make a quick stop for fresh flowers, and my eyes are drawn to a bright yellow mum in the center of a bouquet of burgundy and orange.

The clouds are heavy and drop a few sprinkles on the windshield as we drive west out of the city to our former neighborhood in the suburbs. "This feels tougher this year for some reason," he says.

I ask him to say more, but he is too spent from long hours at his retirement landscaping job to want to delve deeper. This day has never been easy to mark or get through, not even after 25 years. We drive the remaining five miles in silence.

The cemetery is in greater disrepair than when we came more frequently in the early years. The narrow road that passes through it is traffic- and weather-beaten. The ground is lumpier and, disorienting for us, there are many more gravestones than before. We used to turn left and stop at the third tree. Now the third tree has been taken down, so we make a mental note, *the sixth stone down from Hildebrand.*

It's been a while since we've come. As I walk down the slope toward her grave, it plays out like a movie in my head, where the makeup artist applies the passage of time with graying spray, wrinkle lines, sagging jowls, age spots and glasses, and the actors assume the gait of older people. But this is no movie. My gray is colored, I am wearing those glasses, and I waver slightly on a particularly uneven mound of grass. The reality of time grips me. The young mother who once leashed up the family dog and came regularly, who could still do flips off the diving board and jump-splits on the trampoline, is now a senior citizen with arthritis and spinal stenosis. The thought nearly staggers me.

Rob carries a bag of fresh mulch from the trunk of the car and starts ripping out the tough weeds that have grown up around Kelly's headstone, which is now showing the black smudging on its inscription that older ones do. Once he's done, he spreads the mulch evenly around the base.

I lay down the flowers on the mulch, kiss my fingers, and touch her name on the stone. Then I step back to take a photo of the grave and the sky. I text it to our daughters, Lauren in Los Angeles, and Leslie in Baltimore, telling them that just as I took it, the clouds parted a little to reveal a bit of sunlight.

"How cool," Leslie texts immediately. "Sending my love... *(heart emoji)*."

"Love that you went to visit her grave," Lauren joins in. "I'm glad you're there *(heart emoji)*."

I take another photo, a close-up so they can see the flowers. But what they notice is the fresh dark mulch instead. They know their father.

Lauren: "Did you also bring mulch? *(heart emoji)* Still tucking her in."

Leslie: "That is def some fresh mulch."

I read the text thread to Rob. He nods and says softly, "Always."

I want to cry. They understand something that has eluded me all this time. In the beginning, the harsh, repetitive swoosh of the clippers as he went around her tombstone cut into my mournful reverie. "Don't do that when I die," I would say, agitated. But the years have softened me. I see now the way he cares for plants, trees, soil—everything outdoors. It's his way of love. And sometimes there are no other ways.

When Kelly lay in a coma in the hospital on the last day of her life, Rob whispered in her ear that it was okay to let go. "We'll catch up to you," he said, his voice breaking as he kissed her forehead, "as soon as we can." At the time, we had no idea how interminably long and crushing the early years of grief would feel, or how imperceptibly, one after another, they would accumulate into a quarter of a century.

We buried Kelly two months after her eighth birthday. Rob was 41, I was 40, Lauren was 15, and Leslie was 12. Can it really be that we've grieved her loss over three times the number of years that she lived with us?

Almost every newly bereaved parent I meet will invariably look at me with the saddest eyes in the universe and ask, "Will it ever get better?"

I usually respond, "It takes time." But what I can never bear to break to them is how *much* time. Like it or not, nature keeps folding day into night into day. Unless you completely drop out of the human race, you choose to end your life, or you actually *do* die of a broken heart—it's a rare, but real phenomenon—you don't have much of a choice except to get up off the couch and put one foot in front of the other.

I once talked to a father whose teenage daughter had died seven years before. When he learned that I was three years into my bereavement, he said, "Oh, you're still very early in the process."

Very early? My heart sank. How much longer would this take? How much worse was it going to get? I thought I was doing better not crying every day. I thought I was moving along.

I often thought about the well-respected stages of grief—denial, anger, bargaining, depression, and acceptance. I couldn't recall ever being in denial exactly, or being ostensibly angry. How long was the depression phase supposed to last? How soon would it be before I could accept all this? I wanted to put my finger on something, like "You Are Here" on a map in an unfamiliar city, or a signpost in a marathon telling me there were only three miles left to go. But it was impossible to do. I was all over the map, and the course, all at once.

Just as many others have done since Elisabeth Kübler-Ross first wrote about the stages and her work with terminally ill patients in *On Death and Dying* in 1969, I misunderstood that those stages were neither meant to help tuck messy emotions into neat packages, nor intended for people to follow them like stops on a timeline—or, even to experience all of them at all. They were simply meant to identify responses to loss that many people have. But because no loss is the same, no response is either.

All I knew was that I was frantically trying to *get someplace*. Where was I trying to get? Out from underneath the felled log that crushed my chest, there was no question. Past the blinding pain of my broken heart, for certain. To heaven to reunite with Kelly, most desperately.

Just like people don't necessarily follow the stages of grief in linear fashion, I didn't graduate from one year so that I could close the door on its sorrow and move with less of it into the next. Year Two was harder and colder than Year One. In certain moments, Year Eighteen could thrust me back in time like it was Year Three. Sorrow didn't empty out of my heart like sand through an hourglass. It permeated my cellular structure and transformed me.

The people we love, and have had to say final goodbyes to, continue to populate our memory in pockets, shadows, flashbacks, and floods for the rest of our lives. They are part of the essence and fabric of our lives; we wouldn't ever want them to stop being that. I cried a lot less as the years went on, and I learned to bear the sorrow with more serenity. But I never got *over* or *past* it. Death ended her life; it didn't end my relationship with her.

People will say that a terminal illness or death puts life "in perspective." While what we were going through may certainly have done that for others, *we* were getting slammed way out of it. Our family was now living life in a great distortion of what we knew as routine and normal.

Perspective comes much later, well after the traumatizing event, and there isn't a magic point when you officially "have" it. You have some perspective one week after a death, and you have much more 10 years later. But as I continue to meet newly bereaved parents along the way, it was the quarter-century mark that compelled me to reflect more deeply for their sake. What toll *did* all this truly take? How did we honestly manage, and what have we learned? Were we cheated out of the life we were supposed to have, or were we given the life we were meant to have? Was Kelly's life snuffed out prematurely, or did she live a full life?

In the first weeks after she passed, I longed for the company of somebody with more than a little perspective. In my circle of acquaintances, I personally knew no one with that kind of longevity, except for one woman who happened to mention to me (before Kelly was even born) that she had a daughter who had died 25 years before. We weren't particularly close friends. But I was drowning—and unfortunately too weak to signal her attention to jump into the surf to help me.

A year later, I met another woman who, 23 years after the death of her baby, told me that God had finally "cured" her grief, which made no sense to me at all at the time. I felt like she stepped into the elevator to go to the top floor and shut the door on my nose.

Kelly died in 1993, 11 years before Facebook came onto the world stage. Now, it's a different culture, of course, with social media support groups and instant connection to thousands of people and the events in their lives. There is also much more openness to discussing grief and so many more resources. But is our culture really any better at grieving because of them? And would sorrow have been any less painful if we'd had all that back then?

I could imagine appreciating the ability to find companionship in the darkest moments of the night, checking in with private online support groups, or getting validation for my raging emotions from some of the truly wonderful websites that exist right now. But would I have been comforted by broken heart, praying hands, and tear-streaming emojis, along with "R.I.P. Kelly Bair" comments scrolling by, only to be followed by the same people posting funny videos, vacation photos, and political rants? Would the endless stream of "You're strong! Think positive! You've got this!" gifs and inspirational memes have helped during her illness?

What would I have done to respond to a multitude of other people's stories and concerns when I could barely handle my own?

You don't need several hundred likes, compassion hearts, and cursory well wishes that quickly scroll away, or friends who aren't there for you if they don't happen to be online when you need them. The more *isn't* the merrier. What I really needed were a few people who knew how to listen and love, who got me up off the couch to take a walk, or wordlessly rubbed my feet when I didn't even ask for it, and who let me feel the emotions appropriate to my context and timeline.

Life coaches and spiritual directors call it "holding space" for another person when you listen without judgment, let go of control, let the person guide you where they need to go, and simply give them your unconditional support. In the beginning, friends who knew how to do that were the people I needed. I had room for few else.

Fourteen years after Kelly died, the pastor at the church where I was serving in music ministry at the time brought a young couple up to my office. Robed and rushing to get to the next service, he thrust us toward one another and said five words, "You three need to meet." Gregg and Susan Hurley and I hit it off immediately and so strongly that they invited me that very afternoon to a cancer benefit dance recital in which they were performing.

There, they performed an original dance called, "Two Halves Make a (W)hole." Over the course of six minutes, they danced a love story in two parts. In the first part, they playfully knocked about as a young couple in love. Then Gregg got down on one knee, and they zipped their sweatshirts together in an act of commitment. Still zipped together, they danced with affection and frustration, like any couple. Then the music dramatically changed, and Susan suddenly slipped out of their combined sweatshirt and slid to the floor, disappearing into the shadows. Gregg thrashed about in agony, shock, and bewilderment, then collapsed to his knees, rocking back and forth at her grave, hugging her clothing to his chest.

This dramatic and unexpected ending tore me to shreds. I was wrenched with emotion. At dinner with them afterward, I asked, "What happened in your life to make you understand grief this astutely? I lost a daughter 14 years ago, and you got it exactly right."

He put his fork down, then quietly said, "I just listen and learn."

I learned something, too. His choreography had drawn out and embodied my sorrow so pitch-perfectly, that I began to view grief not just as an endless hemorrhage, or a malady to be healed from, but as a bright, physical, intuitive, loving being *independent of myself*, sent to partner with me in my sorrow.

I asked Gregg to read an early draft of this manuscript. Now Associate Professor of Dance at Messiah University, he remarked that he noticed that I related to grief as a bully partner in the beginning. "It's like the TV show, *Dancing with the Stars*," he said. "At first, you're a complete novice with the pro. You aren't used to being held or led by them, and you don't trust you're capable of doing the things they ask of you, so you resist at first. Every day is a rehearsal, and you groan at the rigor and pain of pulled tendons, bumps, bruises, cracked and blistered feet, and endlessly long sessions. It takes a long time before trust builds, so that you can move together in unison." That analogy made elucidating sense to me. It gave me a grounding, purposeful picture of a process that can feel wild, senseless, and frightening.

By the time I was 21, I had lost all four of my grandparents. Since Kelly's death, I've lost my brother, my parents, my in-laws, and two close friends. But it was my daughter's illness and death that were, by far, the most rigorous training ground for grief that I have ever known, and the compelling experience that called forth this book.

Rest assured at the outset, that while the first years were the hardest, and will receive more attention in my writing, the years since haven't just been one dark vale of tears.

There has been plenty of joy and much laughter as well. But Kelly's illness and death were a crucible from which I have emerged a different alloy. I am irreversibly transformed by her passing. My natural mercy for suffering people has turned to bone-deep empathy. My optimism about life in general has been taken down a notch. I live with a low-grade fear of more bad things happening. I'm more realistic, less caught in my illusions.

At the same time, there is an aquifer of hope and joy that rises up more often than not. It makes life so alive with wonder and holiness that I feel like those who have passed on aren't as far away as we think, but rather that heaven is with us here and now. I feel it in the simplest things—in a beautiful waking dream, in my sweet neighbor's toothless grin, in the waning amber light on the buildings to the east of us, or a dog who makes eye contact with me on a busy street and validates my presence when no one else does.

I feel heaven, as well, in the great swells of compassion that rise up in me on behalf of others I learn of who are freshly facing grief and, most acutely, those who have suffered the loss of a child. I have cried inconsolably for the families of children downed in mass shootings, natural disasters, and from starvation or other causes equally horrific, senseless, and anguishing. Even as I can't imagine those families can ever reconcile their tragedies with a loving God, I sense that my empathy for them comes from a divine place much deeper than I.

We heal by exchanging our stories and discovering we're not so alone in our pain. If you are drowning in sorrow right now, or walking beside someone who is, I hope, from what I share and have gleaned from my family in writing this, that you will find camaraderie in your pain. Perhaps you will discover a Sherpa to guide you along an excruciating, uphill path.

They say losing a child is the worst of deaths and the most punishing of griefs. My purpose is not to refute or defend that. I only want to be for you the person I desperately longed for in the beginning—someone with perspective.

I offer you a messy quarter-century's worth.

CHAPTER TWO

Her last day

The fear is for what is still to be lost.
—JOAN DIDION

If not for the date stamped on our boarding passes, we might never have come home. For five days, we had been in a bubble of happiness. It wasn't that we didn't think at all about what we were dealing with—in fact, it was the foreboding undercurrent of our lives for 15 months and, most ponderously, since Kelly's MRI just four weeks before. But few can retain an anxious grip on their sad circumstances when they're a thousand miles from home, swept up in a cloud of joyful hospitality, treated like royalty, and greeted at every turn by smiling, brightly-colored, costumed characters. It wasn't called The Magic Kingdom for nothing.

There were a couple warning signs on our trip, to be sure. Kelly awoke with a brief headache our first morning there. And on the last night of our trip, she was mysteriously hypersensitive to my touch in the swimming pool.

But otherwise, our family of five was in perpetual motion, making the very best of the very worst of times.

Fifteen months before, at the end of first grade, Kelly had been diagnosed with a large tumor located next to her brain stem. Because the surgeon was able to entirely resect it, we were told she had an 80% chance of surviving five years. But just as we were rounding the bend to finish the first year of radiation and chemo, the 20% got the upper hand in the fight.

A routine MRI revealed four new tumors, two small ones on top and at the back of her head, and larger ones on either side of her head in what the doctors called the "silent" part of the brain—which is why she didn't yet have any symptoms. When we met with the team at Children's Hospital of Philadelphia and saw the scan for ourselves, our hearts shot to the floor. We could see that more surgery wasn't an option. They said that chemo would buy her a couple more months, but that it would, of course, diminish the quality of her remaining days.

"You have some time," her local oncologist at Hershey Medical Center said a week later. "If you haven't done it yet, now's the time to take a trip as a family."

Other oncology families had told us about the fun they had had on their Wish trips. How else would we be able to organize a trip this quickly, ease passage through long lines, and still be close to medical help if we needed it? The doctor didn't pull any punches. "Let her start the first week of school, then take your trip the next week. If you wait any longer, you might regret it."

As soon as we called them, Make-A-Wish flew into action to contact Give Kids The World Village, the accommodations and connecting arm to Disney World for critically ill children and their families. This would be a "rush" wish trip, and they bent over backwards to fit us in. The doctor put Kelly on an anti-seizure med and armed us with heavy-duty pain pills to take with us, just in case.

"Get a wheelchair for your child," they told us after breakfast our first day at the Village. "Disney World is tiring for healthy people. Don't exacerbate your child's weariness by making them walk."

At first, Kelly had fun pushing her sisters around in her wheelchair. But wilting quickly in the intense heat, she gratefully rode around in it the rest of our time there, getting out of it only to go on rides, to eat, and to swim.

All too quickly, it was late afternoon on Sunday, September 19, 1993, and as the dread of her uncertain future crept back into the picture, we squeezed every last drop out of our trip in a grand gesture of denial. At Sea World, bent over a limpid pool of trilling and squeaking dolphins, Kelly splashed the water with her fingers, thrilled when the fleshy length of a large bottlenose arched and brushed up against her palm.

A few hours later, we claimed our seats on the plane, and since this was eight years prior to the tight airline security we know now, Rob got up to ask the pilot if Kelly could see the cockpit. I was chatting with Lauren and Leslie about school the next day when we heard a click and the fuzzy static of the intercom. "Hi, Mom," came Kelly's voice, followed by a little giggle.

By 7:00 p.m. we had reached cruising altitude, and the flight attendants moved through the aisles to hand out supper trays. Kelly ate a full dinner as we gazed at the beauty of a sunset from 36,000 feet. After the two-and-a-half-hour flight from Orlando to Baltimore, she conked out with her sisters in the van on the 90-minute drive home to Lancaster, Pennsylvania.

At 11:45 p.m. we pulled into our garage, and Rob scooped Kelly up into his arms and carried her into the house. She woke up when she heard the excited patter of our two-year-old sheltie Tucker's paws against the floor as he squealed to see us. She smiled sleepily, dropped to her knees to embrace his squirming neck, and buried her nose in his fur. "Oh, sweetie, I missed you." Then Rob carried her up to bed behind her older sisters. The next day was a school day, after all.

He came back down to unload our suitcases and had no sooner gotten them all into the kitchen, before we heard Kelly groan. We raced upstairs to find her sitting on the edge of her bed. Suddenly, eyes wide with panic, she clenched her head and screamed, "My head hurts!"

I ran for the emergency medicine and returned with a glass of water and a plastic basin. My hands trembled as

I fumbled to open the bottle and shake out the pills that, mercifully, we hadn't had to use while we were away.

She swallowed the pills, then immediately and forcefully vomited. I cradled her in my arms, and she moaned softly for a minute or two as the pain dissipated. Then she relaxed and let me lower her down into her pillow, where she closed her eyes and promptly fell asleep. It was midnight after all, and she was exhausted.

Lauren and Leslie appeared in her doorway. "Is she okay?"

"I think so," I whispered. "Just a really bad headache this time. Go on. Get some sleep now."

Rob and I collapsed into bed 20 minutes later, utterly spent. "I better check her one more time," I said, climbing back out of bed.

There was a mild gagging sound from her throat, and she tugged at her waistband. I immediately turned her on her side. "Do you need to vomit again?" When she didn't wake up, her breathing quiet and even, I brushed the tender new growth of hair off to the side of her forehead, kissed her, and went back to bed.

"I feel like I should stay with her," I said.

"You'll hear her if she needs you," Rob assured me. "These could be long days ahead of us. You're gonna need your sleep."

For a long time, neither of us could speak. I could hear Rob crying softly, as I was, too. "Lord," he choked. "If you have to take her—*please*—take her quickly. I can't bear to see her suffer."

I heard a thud during the night. Thinking it was Tucker rolling over and bumping the wall in his corner at the bottom of the stairs, I went back to sleep.

In the morning, Rob tapped my shoulder. "Lisa, wake up. I need you to help me. Kelly fell out of bed last night. Let's move her into bed with you."

I followed him to her room, where Kelly lay stretched out on the floor on her back. "She's really chilly," I whispered, rubbing my hand across her bare legs, wishing I'd put more than a T-shirt on her the night before. Why hadn't I gotten up to check the noise I'd heard during the night? We had come, in a matter of hours, from sticky Florida weather in the mid-90s to the first invigorating coolness of fall. How long had she lain there?

After warming her with me in bed for a while, I got up and went downstairs to help Lauren and Leslie get ready for school. "I can't believe she hasn't even stirred," I said to Rob. "I've never seen her this worn out."

In front of the hallway mirror, Rob tugged at his shirt collar and straightened his tie. "I could've used a few more hours of sleep myself."

I fumbled in the desk drawer till I found the booklet of school excuse slips. Tucker banged his nose against the wooden slats of the blinds on the back door. "Tuck, I'll let you out in a minute," I said, scratching a ball-point pen across a tablet to get the ink started.

"Mom, is Kelly okay?" Lauren asked, coming into the kitchen.

"I don't know. I guess she's just exhausted. The trip was tiring for *us,* and we're healthy."

I handed the girls their excuse slips and let the dog out. Afterward, I went upstairs to check on Kelly. "It's strange," I said, coming back downstairs to Rob. "She's so still it's almost like she's—in a coma or something."

"Is Kelly in a *coma?*" Lauren looked startled.

"I don't think so. But we'll have to wait and see how she does in the next couple of hours."

"Lauren, the bus is coming!" Leslie called from the living room.

"Bye, you guys have a good day!"

"Mom, get Tucker inside—he's following us!"

Tucker bounded back inside and slurped water from his bowl, scattering drops all over the floor. He scampered over to Rob, who stood at the counter, laying sliced meat on sandwich bread.

"Are you sure I should go to work?" Rob asked. "What if things aren't okay?"

"I'll call you if they're not. I'll let her sleep longer, and then see how she is."

"You don't think I should stay here?"

We lived only a five-minute drive from the school. "No, it's okay. I'll call you either way in a couple of hours."

When everyone had gone, I went upstairs and put a load of clothes in the washer.

After 30 more minutes and she hadn't so much as stirred, I pulled back the covers to try to rouse her and saw that the sheets were soaked underneath her. I lifted her eyelids like the nurses had done in the hospital. Her pupils were fixed in a dilated position and didn't contract with the light.

I called the oncology clinic at Hershey Medical Center, where Kelly had gotten some of her treatment. They told me her regular doctor was out of the country, and that the chief oncologist on call was in a meeting and would call me back afterward. I hung up the phone and waited for a moment before calling back to add, "I think my daughter might be in a coma."

Within seconds, the chief was on the line. He listened carefully as I described her condition and the medications she was taking. "There is a possibility that the Dilantin has built up in her system, which could cause her to be comatose," he said. "But the other possibility is that it's the tumors. If it's the Dilantin, she'll come out of it within a day, and we wouldn't treat her here with anything else." He paused, his voice gentle. "It's my understanding that your wishes are not to prolong life with any further treatment, is that right?"

"Yes," I said.

"Either way, since she's comfortable, we wouldn't be doing anything for her here, except to run a blood test and CAT scan. We'd be glad to have you come here, if you'd feel better knowing."

Rob and I agreed we didn't want to weather this alone. Within half an hour, I had washed and redressed Kelly, and

Rob had come home to transport us to Hershey Medical Center. We lowered the back seat of the van and stretched her out over sleeping bags.

The CAT scan confirmed the devastating news: the new tumors had mushroomed in size and were shutting down her organs. We chose not to admit her but drove her home, lay her on the sofa in the family room, and wrapped her in blankets to keep her warm.

Rob picked the girls up from school to prevent them from having to walk straight off the bus, unprepared, into this new scenario. We held vigil for a couple more hours as family and friends came and went till, finally, it was just our family with her.

Around 4:00 p.m., the slight rhythmic lift of her chest stopped. We knelt beside the sofa and fell in a weepy heap on top of her.

After a policeman arrived (required by law to rule out foul play) and our family doctor came and pronounced her death, she lay for five more hours just a few feet from our kitchen table as we somberly ate leftovers from the freezer. We felt slightly comforted that she was still there, like she often was when she felt ill and couldn't eat with us. We had watched her face turn from sallow to bluish-purple so that, by the time the undertaker came at 9:00 p.m., it was clear she had taken complete leave of her body.

But where did she go? And *when exactly* had she gone? Was she hovering over us while in a coma? As we said our goodbyes? Had she been whisked away by angels into eternal bliss, never to look back? One person told me that people on the brink of death sometimes try to walk toward the light. *Had she fallen out of bed while reaching to take the hand of an angel?*

That first night without her, the house had an unsettled energy, as if celestial beings had passed through, and we were left in their wake. Leslie crawled into bed with her sister, and since the protective pad on our bed wasn't waterproof and our mattress had been ruined, Rob and I slept on the floor beside them, our now truncated family of four caught in the liminal, slightly spooky space between earth and the incomprehensible afterlife.

We were staring at the illuminated stars glued onto the ceiling when Lauren broke the silence. "Dad, I'm afraid."

"Afraid of what?" he asked.

"That Kelly will appear to me—and scare me."

"Scare you?"

"Yes," Leslie joined in. "Kelly was teasing us a few weeks ago and said that after she dies, she's going to sneak around and go 'boo' when we least expect it. Will she be able to do something like that?"

We thought of the time she ended a sister tiff by dramatically swinging around the banister on her way upstairs with, "Oh, just let me go to Disney World, and *then* I'll die!"

She was feisty *and* prophetic.

But what powers *did* she actually now have?

CHAPTER THREE

The first week

You must go on, but you can only go slowly…
I stumble forward on bleeding knees.
—REBECCA FABER

The last thing Rob and I wanted to do the next morning was shop for a new mattress. Going out in public so soon required looking presentable, restraining emotion, and forcing social graces. The salesman tried to engage us in friendly conversation, but it was too much work to respond with more than a few words. We made our selection quickly and paid extra for same-day delivery.

When the men arrived to carry out our soiled mattress, I saw urine trickle from the corner of it as they rounded the stairs. My heart broke. *The life of my child slipping away.*

And that's how it felt in the beginning—like memories of her were draining away, siphoning out, or like a strong gust of wind had swept my favorite kite right out of my hands, and I was watching it flutter farther and farther away. I gathered meaningful objects and photos and set up a small shrine on a table in the family room, as if I could stop the siphoning from happening.

In spite of exhaustion, sleep did not come easily. At night, the backs of my eyelids were a movie screen ready to play back every mother regret imaginable. I would watch Kelly clench the sides of her head as her last words, "My head hurts!" thundered over and over in my ears. Then I'd agonize as I watched myself leave her bedside to go to my own that night. The thud when she fell to the floor would amplify in my ears, and I'd scold myself for being so stupid for not recognizing more quickly that she had slipped into a coma.

One night, when the replays were relentless and intolerable, I left our comfortable new bed and crawled into Kelly's. Instantly, I was soothed. Curling up on my side, her teddy bear pressed against my womb, I let the scent of her in her unwashed sheets envelop me. I inhabited her absence and hugged it with my body, sleeping deeply for the first time.

When we were able to drift to sleep together in our new bed that first week, the internal gyrations of grief would wake us up at 3:00 a.m., almost without fail. I would blink awake and not hear Rob's sleep-breathing. "Are you awake?" I'd whisper.

"Yes," came his answer every time. And then the tenderest thoughts of Kelly would bubble up in the quiet, and we'd think of ideas for her memorial service. It was a way to call back all that was spinning away from us.

In 1993, cremation was neither an option in our minds, nor as prevalent a practice then as it is now. It had been traumatic enough to have her skull cut into; I couldn't bear to have her body burned in a furnace. Punctuating all the emotional turmoil during those first couple of days were the phone calls. The funeral director's wife called and asked in a gentle voice, "I noticed that Kelly has chipped fingernail polish. Would you like us to paint her nails?" Two family members called to apologize that they couldn't bear to see Kelly in a casket and may not attend the viewing. Others wanted to know specifics of the interment and in what order we planned to sit for the memorial service. The life insurance rep called to express his sympathy, congratulate us for having had the foresight to take out a policy on each of our children, and ask when he could come over to sit down with us. And so, the transactions of life coaxed us out of the shadows.

At the church on the night of her viewing, tall vintage brass lamps with rose-colored glass shades flanked the ends of her white, youth-sized casket. Kelly lay in her baptismal dress, her white floppy dress hat on her head and a gold cross around her neck. Tucked into the crook of her elbow was her beloved pink teddy bear. She looked normal to us, since we'd spent so much of the last year looking at her in a reclining position, or sleeping. But to others, we were told, it was devastating to see her, even if a surprise and a relief to see us smiling by her side as we greeted everyone.

I was taken aback when some of her young classmates took liberty to lay objects on top of her—flowers, notes, even a framed picture of Elvis. I discreetly shifted them to the side; I didn't want her to get lost under them. But I was so glad their parents had let them come and honor her the way they wanted to. I wondered desperately how the children were faring.

We held a private burial with family and a few close friends in the cemetery just west of our neighborhood the next morning. The memory of it comes back to me in a blur of sounds and colors—the rustling of clothing as people huddled together under the green funeral tent, the reverent cadence of the pastor's voice, Kelly's casket covered in pink and white starfighter lilies and positioned over a yawning rectangle of earth waiting to swallow her whole. Bumble bees swarmed the bouquet, tiny looters oblivious to our pain.

The following evening, the community spilled into the overflow of our church sanctuary, where we brought public remembrance to the life of our daughter, sister, granddaughter, niece, cousin, and friend. There were many tears, but there was also joy, laughter, and transcendent music offered by friends and colleagues.

People buoy you up in powerful ways—especially at the funeral of a child. For a few days, you're like a crowd surfer at a rock concert, held aloft by a power beyond yourself, momentarily anesthetized from the depth of pain you're actually in.

After the service, the girls asked us if they could accept an invitation to go out for ice cream with their friends. We had been through so much intensity together, and they'd been out of school for nearly two weeks. It made sense for them to separate from us and reconnect with their peers.

As Rob and I were getting ready to go home, packing the objects from her memorial table into a basket, I noticed a child from our neighborhood standing at a distance, watching me intently. "Well, hi," I said, looking up. "I'm glad you came tonight."

She inched closer to me. "Mrs. Bair," she said, sober-faced and clutching her stuffed lovie. "Why did you take Kelly's teddy bear out of her casket?"

My face flushed with guilt. I felt like a child caught stealing from a store. This observant young girl had seen the bear with Kelly at the viewing, and now on the memorial table. I could picture her imagining what it would be like to be buried in the cold ground without her one tangible source of comfort. The tenderness I felt toward her crushed me. How could I have been this thoughtless and cruel?

One afternoon, somewhere between that fateful MRI and our Disney trip, we'd had a conversation with Kelly about death and burial. We assured her that each of us is a soul living temporarily in a body, and that our souls go to heaven to live forever with God, but that cemeteries are where our bodies go. Kelly had faith to understand, and even told us her preference between two local cemeteries.

But when she had had enough of the conversation and was turning to go outside to play with her friends, she said, almost as an afterthought, "Oh, and put my teddy bear in the casket with me."

Our family valued that bear more than anything else among her possessions. Rob and I had already talked about how we knew we would need it. Lauren had the same instinct and even privately asked if she could have it. We had solved the dilemma by putting it in the casket with her for the viewing *and* taking it back out to keep for ourselves. But now I felt like I had let Kelly down, too. Before I could think how to respond, the little girl's mother took her by the hand and murmured something about how she shouldn't bother me.

The next morning, my brother called, and then my mother. To each, I poured out my heart about the teddy bear. But instead of the consolation I was hoping for, they both sincerely wondered, "Why *did* you take it out?"

Now I was a wreck about it. I thought I had been through the worst of grief with the phases of her illness. I was naïve to think I understood the depths to which it was now possible to plummet. Once the crowd had set me back down and I was finally alone, the weight of sorrow was so heavy it was like someone had tightened a vise on my heart, then sat down on my chest. Now, the one tangible source of comfort, her teddy bear, had become a source of guilt and even more regret.

I was lying on the couch in the family room, racked with pain over this, when a close friend called and asked if she could stop by before heading back to her home state. "I imagine your house is full of people—"

"Actually, it's only Rob and me at the moment," I said. And then I tearfully blurted out my pain over the teddy bear.

She listened, and then lifted the guilt right off my shoulders. "Lisa, Kelly has Jesus. She doesn't need her teddy bear anymore."

When she arrived moments later, she let herself in through the front door and immediately went to the kitchen, where she reached under the sink to get a pair of rubber gloves. From the sofa in the family room where I was lying, I watched the yellow gloves flash in deft movements as she washed and stacked the dishes before finally peeling them off to hang over the faucet.

Then, with barely a word, she came over to the couch, sat at my feet and began to rub them. I cannot begin to describe the impact of this simple and profound gesture— of not asking me how she could help, but instead just doing what came so naturally to her. When she was ready to leave, she lifted her hand as if to say, *don't even think about getting up,* then left as unobtrusively as she'd arrived.

It was inconceivable to me that Kelly was not going to live in our house or come home anymore. I didn't realize, until we had one less person in our home, how much I depended upon the sound, movement, and whereabouts of all of us coming and going. I knew the times of each of our departures and arrivals, the rhythm and weight of my husband's and children's footsteps on the stairs, the sound of keys being hung, or backpacks being flung. I knew when they were in the bathroom or their bedrooms, and when the patio door opened and they went outside to jump on the trampoline. The family rhythm was now off-kilter. One of us was *away*. Surely, she would come back when all of this was over.

Several days later, I was alone in the house, brushing my hair in front of our bathroom mirror, when a dark shadow suddenly eclipsed the light from our bedroom window through the door behind me. Fear seized me, and I jumped. I turned to see the Mickey and Minnie Mouse helium balloons, given to Kelly prior to our Disney trip, suspended in the doorway.

Somehow, on a day with the windows closed and no perceivable air flow, they had moved from the far corner of her bedroom (where they'd hung and not moved for over three weeks), traveled 10 feet, made a 90-degree left turn to dip underneath her overhead door jamb, another 90-degree to turn right and float down the hall another six feet, before dipping underneath another door jamb. Then they made a 180-degree left turn to dip under yet another door jamb, till they were right there behind me.

Perhaps a physicist could explain this, but how did they come just then *to find me?* I could only marvel and cry as

I read the elegant inscription on the silver mylar foil just under the characters' faces: *Somebody loves you.*

Maybe she wasn't so far away after all. Was this unfathomable distance between us now, in fact, no separation at all? Was she seeing me through a one-way mirror? Or had my own guardian angel nudged the balloons over to where I was, to bring me a creative and tangible sign of God's presence and comfort?

Moments like these take your breath away. But soon enough, I was back on the couch again. Getting up to re-engage with the world when you're blind with grief is like launching a rocket against g-forces into space. The resistance is enormous.

The word "bereave" derives from the Middle English word *bereven*, and the Old English word, *bereafian*, which means "to deprive, seize, or rob by violence." We tend to say "bereavement" in respectful, hushed tones, like undertakers do when they talk to families of the deceased. Or, we choose the sentiment written in elegant gold script on a greeting card—*God bless you in your bereavement.*

But when death has robbed you of your child, even if you're somewhat prepared for it, there is nothing hushed, gentle, or respectable about it. It is violent, clamorous, suffocating, and paralyzing.

It's a wonder anyone gets through it alive.

CHAPTER FOUR

The first month

The human soul doesn't want to be advised or fixed
or saved. It simply wants to be witnessed.
—Parker J. Palmer

It stood out among hundreds of sympathy cards—a simple notecard with a sketch of a house on it, from our neighbor across the street. She didn't try to convince us that Kelly was in a better place, that God thought better of the idea of her as a human and decided she should be an angel or a rose in his garden, or send us any number of other platitudes. She had written a single, heartfelt sentence on the inside: *All I do is look at your house and cry.*

I hugged her right then and there in my heart for getting it right, for not trying to put a bow on a tragic situation or imply how we should feel theologically. I loved her for feeling as much as a human can from outside the bubble of those feeling it the most.

For the last year and a half, we had been saying goodbye to Kelly, one traumatic phase after another: when she was diagnosed six weeks shy of her seventh birthday, when she lost her hair and vitality to chemo and radiation, and when cancer recurred, death was imminent, and anticipatory grief overwhelmed us.

Lauren, 14, was mostly at home the summer Kelly was sick and had gone out of her way with her art and humor to keep Kelly's spirits up. We were going to pull Leslie, 11, out of gymnastics for financial reasons. But our generous neighbors paid for her to keep going that summer, and we agreed routine was probably better for her anyway. Our parents jumped in to help in every way possible, while Rob worked on the summer maintenance crew at the high school, and I stayed weekdays with Kelly in Philadelphia for surgery, recovery, and radiation treatments.

We saw each other mostly on weekends. But we were in one accord—do whatever it takes to keep Kelly alive, get through the treatment protocol, and keep her spirits up in the process. Now, in the first weeks after her death, we were disoriented, in shock, lost, and without purpose.

Rob had already assigned his fall tennis team coaching responsibilities to someone else and now returned to his job as a high school counselor with a personal caseload of over 300 students. In spite of only a three-day bereavement leave for immediate family members in his employment contract, the school had graciously given him a week off to go to Disney World with our family. But like with our girls, once he set foot back into the bustling high school of over 2,000 students, it was akin to pulling a car that shouldn't go over 35 m.p.h. onto a major interstate.

The distraction and focus required in our jobs, and for the girls in school, may have been helpful at some level. But because those g-forces pull hard while you're trying to function during the day, we couldn't help but crash when we got home. Rob described the drive home from school as "entering the climate of grief." He would come in the door, put his things down, and sometimes only murmur, "Bad Kelly day." When I looked into the living room after dinner, I'd often see him lying on the sofa in the dark, clutching her teddy bear to his chest.

For me, it was returning to church choir rehearsals, staff meetings, and everything that goes with administering the music and worship department of a large church. There was plentiful love and compassion from my co-workers. But we all had our jobs to do and a growing congregation to serve. If my colleagues *didn't* ask how I was, I felt isolated, misunderstood. And if they *did*, I didn't always know how to give a short answer to something so unspeakable and overwhelming. Nor did I feel that I had the luxury to indulge my true feelings on the job.

When I wasn't at work, it was back to the couch. A neighbor came over one afternoon and invited me to go for a walk. Her insistence was too strong for my resistance, and she finally got me up and out the door. The physical movement was important, something I couldn't have mustered without her.

Rob would often comment that he didn't know where he was on "the map." Our emotions were jammed up and not free-flowing—like a smartphone navigation map cluttered with dotted and solid red lines indicating slower traffic or standstills because of accidents and construction zones. Some days we were pulled off-road on a detour. Other days we were stalled on the shoulder of an interstate with a white cloth hanging limply from the driver's window. The jolting wind currents of other cars speeding by were punishing enough to knock us over.

I suspect the choir looked at me directing them that first Sunday, just two days after Kelly's memorial service, with disbelief. *How can she stand up here and do this? She's so strong.* Looking back, I should've asked for at least that Sunday off. As it was, we'd already taken off two entire weeks, and now we felt obligated to get back to our jobs. Contractually, Rob had to. The church would most likely have given me more time, had I asked. I didn't, no one suggested otherwise, and I certainly didn't have the emotional wherewithal then to defend my self-care in such ways.

Our girls seemed happier to be back at school than at home with their brooding parents. But both of them had close friends who told them they were so sorry about what had happened, but that they couldn't talk about it—*it was too hard*. So they kept running the high-speed treadmill of their teenage years, their feelings pushed back into hiding.

While my adult daughters will be heard from in more depth later in this book, Lauren told me only recently that she barely missed a beat during those early weeks, except for one soccer practice and a class on death and dying. Her teacher excused her, giving her a pass to go elsewhere, leaving her to feel even more isolated. "Nowadays," she said, "maybe a teacher would've asked, 'How are you doing, Lauren? Are you checking in with anyone about all of this?'"

I regret that we didn't immediately get ourselves to professional family counseling then or, for that matter, during Kelly's illness. Regular sessions would have helped us talk to each other and sort through the stress and tangled mess of our emotions during the 15 months of illness, and for at least two years of acute grief. But even making an appointment requires a level of self-shepherding that we just didn't have at the time.

There were support groups to be found, but the ability to sustain attendance in one of them means (a) that you have to take the initiative to get there, and (b) that the very first connection has to stick. Four weeks after Kelly died, Rob and I were invited to a group for bereaved parents at Hershey Medical Center. But everyone else in the group had been there for well over a year. They had bonded and were at a point where they could laugh about some things. We weren't, and never returned. We did receive some helpful literature in the mail from The Compassionate Friends. But being in a room full of parents who had lost children felt impossible at the beginning. We never managed to get to one of their meetings at all.

There is the brilliant Jewish tradition of *Avelut* (the Hebrew word for mourning). Consisting of three periods, *Shiva*, *Sheloshim*, and the *Year of Mourning*, it releases the newly bereaved from having to figure out for themselves how to maneuver through fresh, debilitating grief when their coping mechanisms are over-stressed. What a help it must be to have that kind of structure at such a disorienting time.

I also once heard of a tribe in a developing nation that practices the custom of tying a band of thick natural twine on the upper arm of those who have lost immediate family members. Until it disintegrates, usually in about a year or so, no extra demands are to be asked of those people. Legend or not, it is a brilliant idea.

People say, "If there's anything I can do to help, please let me know." But it's an impossible request to respond to when you're suffocating from grief. I heard one grief expert liken it to "giving a non-mathematician a very complex math problem and telling them to figure out the answer." You truly need people to think *for you* how to help you, and then to just do it. Or at least give you the opportunity to refuse it. A bereaved person simply doesn't have energy to create ideas to make other people feel useful.

One friend was unusually skilled at offering to help. She called once or twice a week and left messages saying that I didn't need to return her call, but that she was available on certain days in case a need arose. She called so regularly that finally when a need did come up, I asked her to fill it, just because she was so gently persistent and sincere.

Sensitive souls like her were instinctively in tune. Others weren't as much, though I don't question their loving intentions or what they might have felt but couldn't speak. Certainly, friends had preoccupations in their own lives that precluded them from having us at the center of their universe! But the empathic ones gave me the extraordinary gift of presence. They looked at me with eyes that said *I have forever to listen,* and then let me talk, cry, lament, or just be. There is no more powerful help for a bereaved parent than that.

We longed to know how our girls were doing, and to help them express their feelings. But it was early fall, and they were thrust back into the same relentless student traffic Rob was in day after day. Except that they were going right from class and bustling hallways into sports practices and homework. Then on Sundays, there were often soccer tournaments or gymnastics meets, and I was gone with multiple services in the morning and youth choir rehearsal in the evening.

When we did manage to check in with them, we felt rushed to jam deep thoughts into brief spaces. "How are you doing?" was too broad a question. It simply can't be answered when you have no idea where you are in your emotional world, let alone when you are 15 and 12 years old, and the people you're used to going to with your problems are struggling too hard themselves. Words choked in our throats. I misread their reluctance to talk, not realizing they might have been reading the pain in our demeanors and not wanting to compound our distress. We had felt helpless with Kelly, and now we felt helpless with them.

It certainly would have been understandable if, watching us be so consumed with their younger sister throughout the 15 months of her illness, and now in her death, they would have wondered if we would have been less torn up if one of them had died instead. It's an easy conclusion for a child to come to when all the parental energy and concern is flowing almost entirely in the direction of another. For good reason, siblings are often called the forgotten mourners.

Lauren told me recently that her greater worry was that she, too, would die of a brain tumor. She had heard of a family in which two members were diagnosed with them, and this unspeakable fear gnawed at her well into her adulthood. But we never knew this.

We tried to check in with both our girls to reassure them. But we had neither objectivity nor insight to help each other. We were like accident victims lying on the road, desperately caring about each other's welfare. But we each needed too much attention ourselves to be able to help the other.

CHAPTER FIVE

Our changing family

There's no tragedy in life like the death of a child.
Things never get back to the way they were.
— PRESIDENT DWIGHT D. EISENHOWER

When Dwight and Mamie Eisenhower's firstborn son Ikky was three years old, he became gravely ill with scarlet fever. Due to the contagious virus, his parents were barred from visiting their ailing son in the hospital. "Forced to remain outside," biographer Geoffrey Perret writes, "Eisenhower desperately pulled himself up to the window of his son's room countless times, gripping the window ledge to gaze upon his dying child until, strength failing, he fell to the ground."

This future WW II General and eventual President of the United States was on the ragged edges of a breakdown, and would refer to his beloved Ikky's death as "the greatest disappointment and disaster of my life."

Likewise, Kelly's diagnosis created a fault line in our family foundation. Her death now made the plates actively shift, like in a major earthquake. Emotionally, our furniture had toppled, and the ordered contents of our lives had spilled out of drawers and closets.

Instantly, we were vaulted out of the elementary school years. The day after the memorial service, Lauren got asked out on her first date. A few days after that, Leslie got her first period. No more toys to buy for birthdays and Christmas. Did we still have three children, or just two, and was Leslie now our youngest child?

It would happen again and again in the first months, and forevermore after that. A friendly clerk in a department store would say, "Oh, this is such a cute top. Is this for your daughter?"

"Yes."

"How nice. And how old is she?"

"Twelve."

"Do you have other children?"

"Yes, two other daughters."

"Three daughters, what fun! What are their ages?"

"Fifteen, twelve, and—"

I quickly learned that my answer could stop conversation cold, especially in the beginning when it was only weeks or months since she passed. But I could not *not* mention Kelly. I didn't suddenly delete her from my life like bananas on my grocery list. To say I had only two daughters felt disrespectful to her existence and to our family. I decided early on that my answer would always be, "I have three daughters. My youngest passed away."

Kelly's death confirmed that the great family disturbance we hoped would be temporary was now permanent. There was nothing normal about anything. It was desperately hard for us to find each other in the mess, let alone communicate. The instinct can be to run from or close the door on everything that hurts.

Meanwhile, we felt like Kelly was a missing person, and our job was to find her. Rob and I searched for her everywhere—in the faces and hair of other children, on TV programs and in magazines and calendars that arrived in the mail. We worked to find Kelly in crowds, radar-locking on any blond kid whose physicality even somewhat conjured her up. One of us would spot a child who was so close to her likeness that we'd elbow the other to look, and then stare endlessly, willing her back into our world.

Ted Rynearson, M.D., Clinical Professor of Psychiatry at the University of Washington, says, "You can almost liken grief to an amputation. When an important part of ourself, like a close family member or friend is dis-membered from us, we re-member the presence of that person as a phantom presence. And we go through an involuntary process of trying to reattach with somebody that we've been amputated from."

I'd go to our bathroom one or more times a day and open the drawer where I kept the sliver of blue soap that Kelly had taken to cancer camp the week we learned of her recurrence of cancer. I'd close my eyes and inhale it like an addict, trying to bring back the feel of her skin next to mine.

Tucker was looking for her, too. Every weekday at 4:12 p.m., he'd hear the school bus brakes screech to a halt at the stop sign at the corner and go to the window, squealing with excitement. When she didn't come, his eyes would anxiously trace the path from the bus to our door over and over again. For a few days, I'd go out on the front stoop and torture myself along with him. I'd look underneath the bus, willing her little legs with white socks and sneakers to step down once more onto the pavement on the other side of it, then her body to come around the front of it into full view.

I soon stopped doing this, but Tucker kept it up for six weeks, until I couldn't bear it anymore. Finally, I scolded him. *"TUCKER, STOP! SHE'S NOT COMING HOME ANYMORE!"* Then I burst into loud, awful sobs, because I had just broken the news to myself, too.

A boy in Lauren's grade knew of our family's circumstances, and he waited as long as he possibly could. But time was running out. The day after the memorial service, he finally called to ask Lauren to the homecoming dance. She was delighted to accept. When she and I could finally get it together to shop for her dress, it was just five days before the dance. The shopping was a fun, much-needed distraction for the two of us, and Lauren quickly found a dress she liked at a department store.

But she wanted to try some others on, too. We went to a special occasions dress boutique, where she fell even more in love with another. But it was too loose at the top. The owner whipped out her tape measure and snapped it around Lauren's waist. "You can alter the dress this quickly?" I asked.

"Of course. No problem," she said.

The day before the dance, we went back to pick it up. But when we got home and Lauren tried the dress on again, it was still gaping at the top. Since the boutique had closed for the weekend, and I wasn't ready to have her use safety pins for a nice evening out, I didn't see another solution except to return to the department store and buy the first dress.

The following Monday, when I went to return the ill-fitting dress, the owner told me flatly, "Once a needle is put to a dress, the sale is final. I can't refund your money."

"But you measured her, and it didn't fit," I argued. "We didn't have any other choice."

She wasn't about to budge or take responsibility. Later that afternoon, I wrote her a letter so I could explain what our last two weeks had been like. I had hoped for a little understanding. But she wrote a letter back saying this would be the first of many special occasion dresses for my daughter, that I needed to get over all my emotion about it, and that, under no circumstances, would she return our money.

I leaned against the doorway of Kelly's room, clutching her letter like a knife to my heart, sliding to the floor in tears. A solid-hour cry there on the floor wasn't just about the dress, I realized when I finally got up.

These days, when Leslie gets overwhelmed caring for her three kids, she sometimes says she has no bandwidth to deal with anything extra. Grief is like that. It takes rapid control of every frequency used in the transmitting and receiving of energy and leaves little reserve for anything else.

We heard that some people told others that we were "strong and full of faith"—frustrating to hear, because an assessment like that is based on superficial information. All they were seeing was any one of us at a given time walking around showered, dressed, and functioning, perhaps even laughing or smiling occasionally because the business of life in the daytime mercifully distracts you somewhat from your interior life.

But in the evening when we returned home, exhausted from holding it together, we collapsed into our private sanctuaries where we could nurse our grief. Rob and I had lost time with the older girls during Kelly's illness, and now we were losing time in their critical teenage years, just attending to the massive hemorrhaging of our hearts.

Grief needs all your attention. Right after your child passes, it's your main job. You *must* tend to it like you would a broken leg, an inconsolable baby, or a heart attack. If you don't, and you move away from everything that reminds you of it, or you shove your feelings in a drawer, your subconscious will go to work on it without you. And then when the day comes when something finally pushes all that energy to the surface—and trust me, it will, because it *will* wait for you—look out.

CHAPTER SIX

Grief on the move

*You surrender to being moved through the
landscape of grief by grief itself...
To stiffen, to resist, and to fight it is to hurt yourself.*
—ELIZABETH GILBERT

Two years before Kelly was even diagnosed, we were sold on a pricey reverse osmosis water filtration system. The perky saleswoman sat at our kitchen table, laid out glossy brochures, and waxed on about the wonderful taste of filtered water and its multitudinous health benefits. As she was about to seal the deal with us, one thing she said stuck with me: "Studies even show that drinking pure water helps prevent brain tumors."

We had no reason to imagine such a thing ever happening in our family, but her pitch was effective. We purchased it on a monthly installment plan and marveled at our crystal-clear ice cubes and the delicious taste of our drinking water.

But four years later, just a few months after Kelly passed, I paid the monthly invoice and muttered to Rob, "Gosh, shouldn't this thing be paid off by now?" We had lost track of so much during the whole cancer phase, and now we were only beginning to realize how much we had let slide. I called the next day to inquire.

"The reason you're still paying," the customer service rep explained, "is because you're renting the system."

"*Renting* it?" I asked. "We *purchased* this."

"No," she insisted. "Our records show you're renting."

My best calculations showed that, to date, we had paid $1200 for a $600 system. I could feel my face burn. "You mean to tell me we've paid twice its value, and we *don't even own it?*"

"That's correct."

Just like that, the great dam holding back my grief crumbled, and all I'd politely held at bay for everyone else rushed into the public space like a tsunami. I burst into loud, unapologetic sobs and choked out in an angry, garbled voice, "Do you know your salesperson actually sold us on this system, citing studies saying that drinking purified water *helps prevent brain tumors?* Well, you should know that my eight-year-old daughter just passed away from a brain tumor!"

I cried the ugly cry—there was no stopping it.

To her immense credit, she didn't hang up on me. When the noise in her ear finally subsided, she softly interjected, "A good friend of mine just lost her seven-year-old son, so I have a little bit of an idea how you're feeling. I'm so terribly sorry."

I stopped gasping for air, defused by her compassion. "I did happen to notice," she continued, "that we put your file in the wrong-colored folder. It should be in the *blue* folder, because I see now you did, indeed, purchase the unit. It's in the *yellow* one that says you're renting. That's entirely our mistake."

Grief is at the ready for each morning's rigorous session. But sorrow's work can get blocked or re-routed by the demands of life. Anger can serve as a quick taxi ride back to the dance studio again.

I will be first to admit that it's *really hard* to know what to do for a parent who's just lost a child. They are pretty much inconsolable, no matter what you do or say. People who helped me the most were those who could loosen the pressure valve. Even just saying Kelly's name out loud, or remembering something about her, or acknowledging her in any way was a help, because behind that valve is an energy that flows with rushing power. When it builds up, it presses so hard against your chest you feel like you can't breathe. *It wants and needs to move through*, but it's shy about exposing itself. It needs to feel safe, and it needs space.

I'm a highly sensitive person to begin with. But now, it was like there were landmines planted around me. People could so easily and unknowingly step on one and trigger an explosion. One Sunday after services, our church held a lunch meeting off-site for the adults in our congregation, while the kids were fed and cared for back at the church. Before the meal, an announcement was made: "All those with elementary school-aged children may get in the buffet line first."

One mother close to my age sashayed by me, teasing, "Haha, *we* get to eat first! Too bad *you* don't have any elementary school-aged children!" She might as well have taken a knife and plunged it into my heart. When it was finally our turn to get in line, she rushed over to me, her face grave with embarrassment. "Lisa, I'm *so* sorry. I wasn't thinking at all. My comment had to have hurt you deeply. Please forgive me."

People don't mean to be insensitive. They can't possibly know where those landmines are. And far be it from a grieving person to be able to anticipate them either. They catch you by surprise and slam you to the ground for a bit till you can get back up on your feet.

Before Kelly died, Rob and I didn't concern ourselves much with cemeteries. He grew up playing baseball in the large cemetery behind his house. I got my first kiss in the cemetery next to a boyfriend's house. We didn't think much, if at all, about the lives and narratives of the souls lying beneath, or the feelings of their surviving families. Nor did my boss think how it might feel to me, having buried our child just five weeks before, to see his front yard across from the church studded with little tombstones painted with "R.I.P." and decorated with spiders and cob-webs for Halloween.

I knew he wasn't purposely being insensitive. He and his wife had been wonderfully present to us, loving and compassionate. Kelly loved his sense of humor, and he had taken her for a ride on his motorcycle. They even held the distinction of being the only people Kelly sent a postcard to from cancer camp. But Kelly's grave had become a holy place to me. It hurt to think of our daughter lumped into the category of ghosts haunting little kids on Halloween. I suppose I should've chuckled a little about this since Kelly teased her sisters by saying she would sneak around and go "boo" after she died. But I wasn't laughing much these days.

Around the same time, one of my closest friends, a single woman with no children, sent me a humorous card with, "I thought you could use a good laugh right about now." I read her words and burst into tears.

At our first Thanksgiving without Kelly, my father said the blessing over the meal and acknowledged "those who have gone before us"—which was fine, except that Kelly had been gone for eight weeks, and the last person in the family who had died had passed away 12 years before. My heart ached to hear her name spoken. My father was a deeply feeling man; I'd seen him cry many times, including during a family prayer session at the hospital before her brain surgery. I didn't understand why he didn't mention her name.

Megan Devine, psychotherapist and author of *It's Okay That You're Not Okay*, says that "Saying nothing is a terrible thing to do to your grieving person. For the grieving person, it feels like abandonment. So not only have they lost their person, they've lost their people."

Looking back, I'm convinced Dad didn't want to choke up or make us or anyone else uncomfortable before the big holiday meal. But had he feared reminding us of it, he shouldn't have worried. You can't possibly stir something up that's already in rapid boil on the stove and spilling all over the floor.

Most likely, Kelly was on everyone else's minds, too. Probably no one wanted to brush against the scab and cause more bleeding. My sister, who held her eight-month-old son in her arms at that gathering, would tell me years later what an embarrassment of riches it was for her to have gained a fourth child the same year we lost one of our three. It's so easy, when you're swamped with pain, and others have icebergs in their throats when they look at you, to jump to wrong conclusions about what they're thinking.

At church, every now and then someone with deep concern on their face would stop Rob and ask, "How's *Lisa?*" as if fathers are more like first cousins once removed from the pain of their own child's death. One woman even shook her head and said to me, "Oh, I could never go through what you did," and then walked straight past me, as if I'd been uniquely qualified for this, or had a choice.

Some rushed to reassure with the words, "Kelly's in a better place," or "Someday you'll see her again." I hope they're right. But platitudes don't help when you're struggling so hard this side of the veil. It only pushes grief right back into hiding.

One day that fall, I got in my car to head to church for a planning meeting for the Christmas musical production. The pressure to create happiness for others felt impossible and nearly paralyzed me. I turned on the ignition, then screamed at the top of my lungs before I could even pull out of the driveway.

That first Christmas, Rob and I couldn't bring ourselves to decorate our home. Central to my distress was a red-and-green plaid Land's End Christmas stocking with *KELLY* monogrammed on its large white cuff. I couldn't bear to hang it and leave it empty, nor could I bear to leave the nail in the wood with nothing hanging from it.

Lauren saw our inertia and took matters into her own hands. When we walked into the kitchen after a band rehearsal one mid-December night, we were surprised to see the house glowing in candlelight, decorations in place. And there, on the mantle over the fireplace, were *all three* stockings. It was such a relief to my heart. I don't think there was ever even a question in her mind to *not* hang her sister's.

Holidays are brutal in the first year, though honestly, they're not a whole lot different than any other day. But how do you endure the forced merriment of grocery store and shopping mall Muzak, or sing "Away in a Manger" on Christmas Eve, three months after your child has passed—*Bless all the dear children in thy tender care and fit us for heaven to live with thee there*—without breaking into a million pieces? How do you sing "Silent Night"—*Sleep in heavenly peace*—when all you can think about is your child lying in the ground? How do you deal with the holiday photos when someone is so sorely absent from them?

At church after services that first Christmas Eve, when almost everyone had left, I went back to my office to get my things. On my desk was a small box with a shiny, mauve-colored bow. I hung up my choir robe and opened the tiny card on the top. Inside, it said, *God bears our burdens.* I lifted the lid and parted the tissue paper to find a small, honey-colored teddy bear outfitted in a vintage pink dress. It was signed from a husband and wife in the choir. But it might as well have come from the same angel who pushed the Disney balloons out of Kelly's room and down the hall into the bathroom behind me. Not only was it perfectly sized to fit into the top of her Christmas stocking, with its paws perched over her name on the white cuff, but it also came from the same couple who gave Kelly her original teddy bear.

The holidays had pressed me especially hard. I had tried to rise to the occasion so as not to pull focus away from everyone else's happiness. But it was effort I could maintain only for so long. The day after Christmas was as much a relief as it was falling back into the abyss. Grief patiently waited to catch me there.

During the week between that first Christmas and New Year's, the movie *Philadelphia*, starring Tom Hanks and Denzel Washington, was released. I had a visceral response just to the title itself. Philadelphia was the crucible of our lives, the place where Kelly had her surgery and where she weathered a summer of twice-daily radiation treatments and chemo clinic on Tuesdays. It was the city where we learned to navigate the Schuylkill Expressway and urban traffic, all while tending an ill child on the back seat. Philadelphia was now a holy sanctuary of memories. It was the place where we forged new and diverse relationships, walked the streets and took in sights that would brand themselves in our hearts for a lifetime.

The lobby of our downtown theater was crowded the night Rob and I went. After buying our tickets, our eyes riveted on a Ms. PAC-MAN machine against the wall. Not only was the title of the movie evocative for us, but Kelly had played hundreds and hundreds of games of Ms. PAC-MAN while staying at the Ronald McDonald House in Philadelphia. It was practically her seat at the dining table. Radiation had robbed her of an appetite. She would eat as little as 150 calories some days and feel repulsed every time I offered her more food—until she had that lever in her hands and was swept up in the excitement of gobbling up dots and avoiding the ghosts. I'd sit slightly behind her, surreptitiously slipping spoonsful of pasta or applesauce into her mouth.

We dropped quarters into the machine and played three games before the movie, just to feel close to her.

When the film began and the rhythmic, melancholy strains of Bruce Springsteen's "Streets of Philadelphia" began to underscore the camera zooming in on the iconic city skyline, Boathouse Row, and so many familiar street scenes, I wept silently, fully entering the sadness because I knew this was a cradle in which I needed to be rocked.

I let myself be held by it all, by the music, by the main character's decline and eventual death from AIDS, by the mysterious way grief was using this movie to mirror our story and draw out some of the pent-up feelings from the holidays.

I have come to interpret Jesus's words, "Blessed are those who mourn, for they shall be comforted," with new understanding. I don't think it means that endless streams of people will come out of the woodwork to bring comfort. Many will. But I think it has more to do with *leaning into the arms of grief and letting it lead the dance.* Through it, those in deep sorrow will begin to find comfort.

A bereaved parent is left with a bleeding wound, an eternal homesickness. It takes every ounce of loving energy you have to care for yourself.

CHAPTER SEVEN

Numbing the feelings

You're not a bad person for the ways
you tried to kill your sadness.
— HEALTHYPLACE.COM

They say grief comes in waves. But the loss of a child creates relentless waves with more amplitude and intensity than anyone who hasn't gone through it could ever imagine. At Atlantic beaches, you see signs warning of dangerous rip currents that tell you how, if caught in one, to swim parallel to the shore to get out of it. Red flags warn when winds are high and swimmers should stay out of the water altogether.

But losing a child doesn't give you a choice. It's like being thrown into the waves on a red flag day, and then getting caught in one of those rip currents on top of it. You're trying to swim back to the shoreline against a force that, in actuality, can thrust you seaward at a rate of up to eight feet per second, faster than any Olympic swimmer has ever recorded.

I have no problem understanding why his followers panicked when Jesus gave the order to cross the sea of Galilee, then promptly fell asleep just as a sudden, violent storm came up, swamping the boat. I'd have been the first to cry out, *JESUS, GET UP!!! WE'RE ALL GONNA DIE!!!*

While the story says that Jesus woke up, rebuked the wind, restored calm, and gave them a little pep talk about fear and faith, my experience with grief felt more like I was shaking his shoulders for about a year before I could even rouse him. I wanted immediate calm; he was more interested in how the waves would shape my soul.

I thought several times about driving my car into oncoming traffic to calm the storm on my own and hasten my reunion with Kelly. I neither wanted to leave my precious family nor kill someone else in the process. But sorrow at this level is so blinding and consuming, that there are moments when ending it all feels like a rational choice.

I've known parents who have taken sedatives and serotonin boosters to deal with the overwhelming sadness. Others drink too much, take drugs, work too hard, move to another city, or bury themselves in other distractions. One young mother I know turned to her unscrupulous pastor for help, who then took advantage of her vulnerability and seduced her, which she was helpless to resist because she was in such dire need of comfort.

Though I had more in common with Rob than anyone else in the world in all this, it was pretty useless to derive comfort from each other. We were both too needy, and our genders and personalities too different. I had an expectation that we'd be tuned to the same frequency, but it was simply unrealistic.

Because I emote easily, I thought I was dealing with my feelings. But sorrow had overloaded my circuits. I didn't know where to go with my larger-than-life emotions, and I didn't want people to think I couldn't handle my job or was milking more than my quota of sympathy. Several confidantes gently suggested I should focus more on the living, not so much the deceased. But I was like a moth drawn to the light. I was helpless against the powerful surge toward the one I had lost.

Unconsciously, I turned to what I knew best—the sedation of food. I didn't suddenly resort to this, nor did I know then how, by over-indulging refined carbohydrates, I was getting a dopamine rush and triggering a metabolic process that packs on weight. The stress of Kelly's illness, along with my eating lesser quality food in hospitals and waiting rooms, had already added an extra 15 pounds. Compounded now by the inactivity of taking to the couch any time I could, I'd eat a little more here and there to take the edge off, then more and more to stuff the hollowness and stanch the feeling that I was bleeding out. No wonder I gained another 15. I didn't consciously know I was using food to numb my feelings, but I soon panicked and got myself to a 12-step recovery meeting.

I took a seat in a dingy room in the basement of a church I'd never been in before. Large plastic storage bins were open underneath tables spread with pamphlets, books, and literature. Over and over, as folks gave updates on their lives and recovery, I heard the same inviting words, "Welcome," and "Thank you for sharing."

When my turn came, I introduced myself.

"Hi Lisa, welcome," came their collective affirmation.

I said that I'd just lost my child, then promptly overflowed with tears. And here was where I got introduced to the absolute blessing of 12-step programs: *They said nothing.* They didn't tell me they were sorry for my loss. They didn't rush to offer platitudes or grab a box of tissues and shove it into my lap for me to mop up my messiness and get on with living. But they were actively listening. They let me say whatever I wanted to say and be however I was in that moment for as long as I wanted to talk. I didn't go on very long, just said that I suspected I was using food to cope and thanked them for being there.

"Thank you for sharing," they responded in unison. "Keep coming back."

I cannot stress enough what a gift it was to receive this kind of respectful, uninterrupted space. Encircled by people who understood, if not my exact situation, then certainly the coping mechanism, I had a rare moment of self-compassion and awareness. I had correctly been hearing a spiritual call, but I was going to the wrong address (food) to answer it.

I now believe that the spiritual call is from grief itself—heaven, if you will—telling you that you are *found, understood, deeply loved, and cared for.* I believe that the call knows your pain better than you do, and wants to hold you to its breast and rock you like a baby. It invites you to lean into your uncomfortable feelings.

But we are fearful, desperate humans. We panic and medicate before we allow ourselves to sink deeply enough into those feelings. Grief invites you to weed out the immediate fixes that promise comfort, but instead compound your distress. It calls you *through*, not over, under, or around the pain.

Rob's way of coping was to work more. He didn't live in the watery emotional world that I did. His emotions lodged more deeply than mine, veiled behind his introverted, even-keeled temperament. But when he was triggered by something—a particular song on the radio while driving or painting the back porch—he, too, would dissolve into tears. He would tell me how refreshing it felt to cry, and how going too long without doing so would make his soul feel cracked and dry.

I don't know what our girls did to help themselves back then. I knew Lauren kept a journal. Sometimes I went into her room to check it. But then I'd open her drawer and close it again, not wanting to invade her privacy.

Leslie told us she was coached at the gym not to cry when she fell off the balance beam or got frustrated with a tumbling pass. I wonder if that philosophy spilled over into how she handled the distress at home. I imagine her friends at school and at the gym were also a constant distraction from ever getting quiet enough to feel much of anything for too long.

I wish I could remember myself as the ever-supportive mom who was undistractedly present to her daughters in their already challenging teenage years. But I'm pretty sure that's not the way I was. I do remember being deeply concerned about them, trying to coax conversation out of them about their grief. But when they seemed impatient with me, and their words only trickled out, I figured I was pushing too hard. Perhaps I was simply the wrong person to talk to, or it was their way of numbing themselves from their own chaotic feelings.

I'm guessing now they were in an emotional jigsaw puzzle and didn't even know how to find the corner pieces to begin to put the thing together. I'm not sure I did either. I told them to come to me anytime they wanted to talk. But we were in constant motion, rarely eating dinner together because of gymnastics, soccer, meetings, rehearsals, and Rob's coaching or working late. I took for granted they were managing well enough.

We bumped into each other at night in the narrow upstairs hallway, tossing dirty clothes into the hamper between Kelly's bedroom door and the bathroom, or doing laundry. I'd drift into their rooms to check in on them, but the exchanges were brief, as I knew they were trying to finish homework and get to bed at a decent hour.

Tucker would lie in the center of either one of their beds, gnawing a tennis ball or a piece of rawhide, not letting go of his grip on what he was chewing. But he did stop long enough to look up at me in the doorway so that the whites of his eyes showed at the bottom. He wasn't about to spill what was in his locked vault of information about either one of them.

Numbing yourself may be necessary in the beginning, when things are so bleak and raw and you're just trying to survive. But I've learned that what you do to let down your resistance and allow sorrow to *move through* is what genuinely helps you. For me it was a hundred tiny things—like sniffing Kelly's soap or indulging the tears when I spotted her birthday or date of death on a gallon of milk or blueberry muffins at the grocery store. Another time it was asking the family to whom I passed down her clothing to please return the boots she wore to camp because it hurt me more than I had anticipated not to have them anymore.

It can be big things, too, like getting counseling, or hooking into a wonderful support group. But the point is, good grieving gets blocked by quick fixes that numb you and promise relief but, in reality, compound your distress. Each moment of leaning into the uncomfortable feelings keeps sorrow from getting stuck and festering into depression.

We are panicky, paradoxical humans, and sometimes, like me, you do both at the same time—go to a wonderful counseling session to deal with all your uncomfortable feelings, and then stop for donuts right afterward because it raked you too raw and wide open.

A hiker friend of mine took a picture of a sign on the Appalachian Trail that I think is particularly fitting for bereaved families: *No camping next 500 feet. Please allow this fragile area to heal.*

So please, if you can, throw the heavy hikers off your emotional property, and be very, very gentle with your heart.

CHAPTER EIGHT

House of memories

*Child loss is not an event. It is an
indescribable journey of survival.*
—Out of the Ashes/Facebook

Kelly's room was situated on the second story of our house, just above the front door. Her bedroom door opened up into the upstairs hallway, right near the laundry and the girls' bathroom. One evening after dinner, I went upstairs, turned on the hallway light, closed Kelly's bedroom door, and retrieved a load of laundry from the dryer to take to fold on our bed.

Lauren came upstairs a few minutes later, rounded the corner to go to her own room, then did a U-turn and barged into mine. "MOM! WHY DID YOU CLOSE KELLY'S DOOR?!"

Her brow was furrowed, her eyes flashing. "I didn't want to have to keep closing her blinds," I said, trying desperately to read her. "Closing the door at night is just easier."

She swung around, unlatched Kelly's door, and pushed it wide open. "Please, *please*," she said, half-crying. "Don't *EVER* do that again!"

Back then, we sometimes walked on eggshells with each other. But even then, I could recognize the emotional claustrophobia. Grief was moving mightily in her, too, and it had enough blockage during the day for her at school. It wasn't about to tolerate a closed door at night. Pastor David had told me in the beginning, "Don't be afraid to enter the house of memories." In that instant with Lauren, I knew what he was talking about.

In the weeks following Kelly's death, some of the neighborhood kids who jumped regularly on our backyard trampoline learned that we had let a few of her friends pick something from the surfeit of gifts that had poured in for her during her illness. One or two would come and ring the doorbell, ask politely if they could have something of hers, and then come upstairs with me to her room to pick what they wanted.

One day, the mother of one of Kelly's classmates from outside our neighborhood called me to ask if she could drive her daughter over for a visit. I was happy to receive them both in our living room, where her curly-haired daughter got right down to business.

"Mrs. Bair," she said, her big blue eyes radar-locking on mine. "I heard that Kelly died on the couch." With her hand, she brushed the sofa cushion where she was sitting, then riveted on me for confirmation. "Was it this one?"

"No, not this one," I said, slightly amused and oddly re-freshed by her audacity, when almost everyone else those days treated me with kid gloves. "Come with me." I got up and led her to the family room where I pointed to the L-shaped sofa. "It was *this* one."

She looked long and seriously at the couch, then turned to face me. "I heard she drooled a little when she died." She touched the corner of her mouth and swept her finger across her cheek to illustrate. "Is that what happened?"

I had no idea where she got this information. "Yes, that's right," I said, marveling at her skill in coming for-ward with her thoughts, convinced she was headed for a future in journalism or forensic science. She asked me a number of other questions I can no longer recall, before her mother thanked me for my time and said they'd need to be going.

Since Kelly had attended only one week of third grade, and then disappeared from class, I asked her teacher if I could come in and share a video from our Disney World trip. I had a clip of her sitting happily in her wheelchair, waving goodbye to the Magic Kingdom. I thought her class would appreciate seeing it, to give them a little closure.

What I loved was that these children were so open about it all, asking questions about how she had died, not worried a bit about upsetting me. They were grief's mini-dancers. They did what many adults couldn't do—took me by the hand and led me all over the dance floor, saying her name out loud, handling her life, helping me enter her bedroom and open her closet door again and again, so that the death-still air kept moving.

Those children made it easier for us to do the same. Two months later, Rob and I instinctively knew it was time to acknowledge that life had stopped in her room, to repurpose it, and to begin deliberately living and moving in it again.

Standing at quiet attention on the floor in front of her bureau, highlighted by the particular slant of the morning sunlight that streamed into her room, were the brown suede boots with the fancy ties. I hadn't been able to move them as long as I had that nagging feeling that she was on some kind of extended vacation and would eventually return.

Now, Rob and I slowly began to box and bag the possessions we cared most about—her books, games, clothing, and stuffed animals—some to keep, most to give away. We paused to cry when certain items brought too strong a swell of memories to the surface. On my own, I probably would have stopped and drowned in the emotion, taking weeks to finish. But Rob is an organizer, and he shepherded us to the finish in one day.

By the time the sun had become a warm glow reflecting off our neighbor's house across the street, her room had been stripped sterile. It depressed me to watch Rob vacuum the floor and to see this once happily cluttered room look so blank and formal. I looked around mournfully, then lingered on the red crayon marks I had once scolded her for making on the white lampshade beside her bed. *The bedside table.* We'd forgotten to empty that drawer, the last place any of her possessions could be found in the house. I sat down on her bed and started to dig through a myriad of toys, barrettes, pencils, markers, headbands, and trinkets of all kinds.

Then my heart skipped a beat. At the bottom was a black-and-white-marbled composition book. She had journaled often during her illness, and I flipped through it, desperate to see if she might have written or drawn something in it. But the pages sliding through my thumb were blank. Until suddenly I saw something and paged forward to open to it.

There, spread over two full pages in the center of that otherwise entirely blank journal, was a prayer she had written. The date was close to when she'd had a vivid dream of eating with Jesus at a table for two, just three months before her death:

> *Dear Jesus, I really felt much closer to you these*
> *past years, and I still do.*
> *I have felt your presents (sic) more.*
> *I thank you for this time of cancer through the past*
> *year and a half.*
> *It has given me a time to get even closer to you!*
> *I am so excited to come to your kingdom someday!*
> *I don't know anything about what heaven looks like.*
> *I know it's going to be the best place I have ever been!*
> *I can't wait!*

It feels so good to know that I'm in your arms, safe and sound!
I love you so much I can't explain how much!
I couldn't of (sic) gotten through last year without you Jesus!!!
This year I really feel like one of God's mitionaris. (sic)
I feel a mesag (sic) to tell people about God!
It's a very, very, very neat and special feeling!

We sat on the edge of her bed and read it together. It was like receiving a letter from her in her new home. I pictured her lying in bed writing this, the image of Jesus eating with her so stunningly and lovingly vivid. And then I pictured her closing her journal with a gentle smile on her face and tucking it deep in her drawer, unknowingly mailing it to us for another time, from another place. We fell into each other and wept.

In time, we would sell some of her furniture at a consignment shop and install an L-shaped desk in the corner of her room. But her closet remained a holy museum of the precious things we would never part with, and which sometimes I would unpack just to hold again: the light blue denim jumper and white t-shirt I loved to see her wearing; her beloved books; the pencil collection her Pop-Pop had started with her; the white, light vinyl jacket upon which Lauren had illustrated dozens of Kelly's favorite things; the plastic boxes that stored the tiny colorful beads from which she made dozens of necklaces for people in our family. And, of course, her brown boots and her teddy bear.

That day, I could never have imagined leaving that memory-laden house, or wanting to move farther away from the cemetery. But grief would lead the dance, and its persistent and unexpected steps would guide us, 18 years later, to do just that.

If my 40-year-old self could've peered into a crystal ball just then, I would have seen my 58-year-old self enter the house one last time. I would pause at the kitchen sink and tuck a tiny card under a little flower on the windowsill. Tears would flood my eyes because this future me knew things I could not yet possibly understand. An ocean of pathos would flow through my pen in writing just these simple words: *Enjoy your new home. We hope it blesses you to live here even half as much as it has blessed us.*

This older me would then turn to leave, but pause in the entryway to look one last time up the stairs. The sound of my children's footsteps and laughter would be so vivid in my memory that I would half-expect one of them to come down just then. I would want to tell the new owners that this home was extraordinarily blessed and that I hoped they would cherish its story.

And with that, this future me would turn to leave, welling with tears and whispering *thank you* before locking the door for the final time.

CHAPTER NINE

The body's calendar

There are some things we can never assign to
oblivion, memories we can never rub away.
They remain with us forever, like a touchstone.
—HARUKI MURAKAMI

What stood out to me that first January without her is that it snowed every single day of the month. The weather felt like a five-pound bag of ice pressed to my heart. With no headstone in place yet, all I could think about was coldness blanketing my daughter's grave deeper and deeper. One morning, Rob pierced my heart when he told me he'd had a dream in which Kelly called to him from the ground: "Daddy, I'm cold, could you bring me a sweater?"

After quietly celebrating Rob's 42nd birthday in mid-January, we rallied to give Lauren a sweet 16th on February 10, just four days before Leslie's 13th on Valentine's Day. I twisted colorful strands of crepe paper and attached them to the ceiling from the hanging light over the kitchen table. Then I filled the area with gold, fuchsia, and teal-colored balloons, all in a fancy pearl finish, and ordered a cake from our favorite baker down the street. This would all be for later, after a surprise dinner with friends and family at a Mexican restaurant. On the way to dinner, Rob, Lauren, Leslie, and I would pick up Lauren's boyfriend at his house.

With January's snow still piled up around driveways, it was a dreary, foggy Thursday night with a bit of fine mist, enough to make a sidewalk slippery, but not the roads. Rob pulled the van into her boyfriend's driveway, and we saw him open the front door and give us a quick wave before turning to secure it. He walked gingerly down the sidewalk, beautifully wrapped gift in hand, then turned left down the sloping driveway and smiled broadly to see us all. He wasn't more than a step or two from the van when suddenly he slipped like a cartoon character on a banana peel and disappeared from view. We let out a collective gasp.

There is that moment of grave concern, and then, after the person who falls gives the all-clear that they're okay, of inexplicable hilarity. Once he was in the van and we confirmed he wasn't hurt, we couldn't repress our laughter. He was a tremendous sport about it, and at this precious young man's expense, I thank him for reminding us all that even the most somber of grief dances comes complete with a blooper reel.

The late winter thaw came none too soon. As crocuses pushed through ice-crusted mulch, and March winds whistled through our north windows and shook the vinyl siding, I gratefully entered the more reflective Lenten season in my job. But Holy Week too closely matched our circumstances. During the somber Good Friday service, I fought hard to hold back my emotion. Then, in an unexpected moment when the congregation was in a period of reflective silence, I let out a loud, embarrassing gasp. I covered my mouth to hold in my sobs, but I was powerless to stop them. We were marking the crucifixion of Jesus, but I couldn't help feeling like Kelly was on the cross with him.

After Easter, we went to a local shop to choose a memorial stone for Kelly. We had labored ahead of time over the wording, and along with the necessary facts, I wanted the simple phrase from Psalm 23 to be italicized over the top, *Thou preparest a table*, to honor her dream of eating with Jesus at a table for two.

The man helping us showed me fonts we could choose from. He could see my disappointment when nothing seemed quite right for that one phrase. I enjoyed calligraphy, and I quickly sketched the words on a pad for him. "Something like this is what I had hoped for."

He surprised me when he took us back into the workshop and said, "I think we should use your exact handwriting." He gave me a writing tool and a stencil and let me carefully freehand the letters. Weeks later, they installed her monument. I marveled at how beautifully they had reproduced my phrase as her epitaph. For a project as cold as stone, this man had let me warm it with my hand.

Not long after that, I bumped into a woman in the grocery store who had lost her son six months before we lost Kelly. As we compared notes, she said three words that snagged me—*emotional jet lag*. She was a teacher running on fumes and had planned to take a sabbatical.

Like her, I had arrived at an airport in another part of the world, shown up for all my appointments, and started to eat meals and go to sleep in the new culture's time zone. But my heart was stranded at the airport back home. I took from her something I didn't yet realize I could give myself—permission for a time-out. My wheels began to turn for how I might be able to manage this.

When spring officially settled in, I welcomed the sunlight and swelling buds on the trees. But simultaneously, I could feel my anxiety rise as the calendar and the weather triggered significant dates.

The year prior, we had *celebrated* having gotten past those dates. But this year, like cars in a funeral train, they approached the station for a different kind of remembrance. Week by week, the calendar moved me from one car to the next: *April 16th—first symptom; June 17th—Lancaster hospitalization; June 20th—transfer to C.H.O.P.; June 23rd—brain surgery; July 7th—discharge from C.H.O.P.; July 13th— start of radiation,* and so on.

When Kelly was diagnosed two years before, I hadn't known how long the train was going to be or where it was heading. Now there was a known destination, and a kind of inexplicable duty and solace in riding the memories straight toward her death. I wasn't wallowing in sorrow; I was deliberately working to move through it.

While I may have had more of a head for dates than my husband did, or been more inclined to sink into their meaning, for me this became a powerful and necessary grieving ritual every year. Of course, Kelly's birthday and the anniversary of her death were the events when I got off my personal train in order to mark the day with my family. But after a few years, I noticed that my body had a calendar all its own and would start to have exacerbated grief symptoms even before my head could wrap around why.

I would sit in a staff meeting on a late May afternoon six years later in my boss's newly painted office. As the conversation would go on about upbeat topics, I would feel increasingly sad, not understanding why I was being pulled down a dark hole. Finally, it would hit me—*the paint color.* I would recognize it as similar to the walls in my room at the hospital when Kelly was born. I would remember it specifically, because it was distastefully set off by the curtain around my bed, an orange-and-green plaid, slightly repulsive to me, the color of baby food peas and carrots.

This was a revelation to me, how deeply the memory of everything associated with joy and pain was housed in my body and psyche. Triggered by weather, the kind of cloud cover, colors, smells, and scenery, my body kept an uncannily accurate journal. Grief could flip open a given page at any point and replay a scene in vivid detail.

Four years before that, two years after her death, I was scheduled to meet with an orthopedist to evaluate my knee pain. My appointment began with an X-ray. But right after it, I dissolved into crying so hard that, when the doctor entered the examining room, he took one bewildered look at me, handed me a box of Kleenex, and said, "Is there something I can do for you? Would you like to reschedule?"

I wasn't able to explain to him then what I would piece together later. This particular June morning was cool and overcast, exactly the kind of weather it was during the very same week and month when Kelly was transported by ambulance to C.H.O.P., just one street over from this doctor's office. Those triggers, and the cold metal of the machines, had ambushed me and taken me right back to all her MRIs at the hospital.

Three years into my grief, my mother asked me if I could help her make a photo calendar to give as Christmas gifts. She handed me a list of all the birthdays in our extended family and asked me to reproduce and paste them in for her. When I scanned the list, I looked past all the birthdays to the one that *wasn't* there—July 30. I was hurt and timidly asked her if I could add it.

She didn't understand at first. While several in my family had sent me cards on Kelly's birthday, my mother never initiated remembrance of the day to me. Sometimes you want certain key people to just *get* it, not to have to spell it out for them. Eventually I told her tearfully that Kelly's birthday and the anniversary of her death were now more important to me than my own birthday. What I didn't tell my mother was how hard it was every year to celebrate *her* birthday, which fell on the day before the anniversary of Kelly's death. Nor did I let on how I would compartmentalize my emotions and rally myself to make it a special day for her, all with boulders in my soul threatening to pull me to the ocean floor.

I share all of this not to dishonor my mother, whom I adored on earth and still adore to the heavens, where she now resides. I say it only to highlight how convoluted the expectations, comparisons, and expressions of grief can be among those closest to you.

Now, not even through the first year of grief, I began to understand that Kelly's dates were branded more deeply into my body and soul than I realized. But I would learn in the following years that it was even more core than that.

My life would now revolve around the year of her birth and the year of her death, like B.C. and A.D. on the modern calendar. Everything in my life was either Before Kelly's Illness or After Kelly's Death.

CHAPTER TEN

Letting your heart catch up

Creativity is the essential response to grief.
—HENRY SEIDEN

The term, *emotional jet lag* played like an earworm in my head over the next weeks. Because my nature is never to impose on anyone or become a burden, I asked for a one-month sabbatical, without pay, at a time of year (July) when I felt the church could more easily manage without me. It was granted.

On Wednesday, June 30, 1994, in the middle of the painful procession of anniversary dates, I came home from work feeling like a hundred pounds had been lifted off my shoulders. In three days, Rob and Lauren would head to a work camp in Appalachia, and Leslie would go to the beach with her best friend's family. They would all be gone for a week, and Tucker and I would have the house to ourselves.

My first two days off, I helped everyone organize, shop, and pack. But I also spent time learning the new computer we had just gotten—our very first *Macintosh*, as it was called back then. I would learn how to email later; right now, I only wanted to figure out how to start a word processing file. My plan was to start writing the book that had ignited a pilot light in my soul and taken shape in my mind even before Kelly passed.

I said goodbye to my family early Saturday morning and went promptly back upstairs to Kelly's small 10x12 room, now repurposed into a combination guest room and office. The empty house, the big beige hunk of a computer, and her bed with its bright floral bedspread all felt like a table set for a holy meal. I laid my journals beside her teddy bear, twirled the vertical plastic rod on the blinds to reduce the glare on the computer screen, and sat down in front of it. I clicked open the file I had designated for my manuscript and stared at the blank, grayish-white screen. An unexpected film of tears washed over my eyes. *Thank you*, I whispered, then typed the title I had known for a year that I would call the book—*A Table for Two*.

I clicked along with ease, the keyboard so much faster and more gratifying than my old electric typewriter: *Dr. Warren led me into the hospital conference room and closed the door.* I quickly pressed *save*, so I wouldn't lose this precious outpouring. I marveled that I didn't need correction tape anymore, and mulled over, as I cut and pasted sections of the manuscript, how fitting the new term, *word processing* seemed.

It felt so completely right and healing to be birthing this book in her room, in the month of her birthday, at a desk in the very same corner where I had once slept in her sheets with her teddy bear. It didn't take long before I wasn't aware which was flowing more freely, my tears or my words.

For one solid week, I wrote 12 hours a day—with breaks only for meals, shopping, and sleeping. I stored chapters on green and yellow floppy disks so they wouldn't accidentally disappear into the ether.

On a midweek morning, I drove to a roadside produce stand and bought fresh summer beefsteak tomatoes and a pint of miniature patty pan squash and sautéed them in butter for lunch, just like my mom used to make. I was eating better than I had since Kelly's diagnosis—actually mothering myself for a change.

With the great gift of my sabbatical, my memories and sorrow now flowing freely onto the page with bottomless permission to express them, I didn't feel the need to eat to numb myself—only for nourishment. I was answering heaven's call. And like a compassionate doula, grief stood by me and supported the delivery.

When my family returned the next week, I was well into the book and continued to write, but not quite so feverishly. Still, by July 30, what would have been Kelly's ninth birthday, I had finished two-thirds of an entire manuscript.

That morning, we ate glazed donuts with the girls in Kelly's memory. One of the few foods she would eat during chemo, we often went to great lengths to get them for her. Memories of last year's birthday, when Rob's sister had dressed up as Minnie Mouse to entertain a group of Kelly's friends, rolled like a bittersweet film in my memory. Back then, we hadn't a clue that her eighth birthday would be her last.

There was no Pinterest or social media to suggest other ways to mark her birthday or the anniversary of her death. We were breaking ground to figure out what we needed to do. This was all that felt right. It was enough, and a relief, just to get through the day.

When I stepped back into my job in August, the internal pressure of grief was noticeably lighter since I had been pouring it out in my book for four weeks. But it wasn't long before August 13 rolled around, launching a whole new level of immersive pain.

One year prior, Rob and the girls had driven Kelly to Philadelphia for a routine MRI that day. I had company and had stayed at home. Later that afternoon, after my friend left and my family had returned, I was just about to doze off on the couch when the phone rang. Kelly was upstairs and heard someone from C.H.O.P. leaving a message on the answering machine. She shouted downstairs for me to pick up. I took the call in the dining room, not realizing she was perched on the stairs, listening.

I don't know whether she could hear the other side of the conversation, since the doctor was in the process of leaving a message when I picked up. But I'm sure she heard the fear in my dry throat as my body reeled against what I was hearing, and I repeated back to confirm, "There are *four* new tumors, and one of them is *hemorrhaging,* is that what you're saying? And we need to go to the hospital *right now,* is that correct?"

At some point, Kelly ran upstairs. I found all three of the girls in Leslie's room, huddled together on the bed, crying.

Now, a year later, a hundred moments from the hours after that phone call flashed back: the desperate drive to Hershey Medical Center, the mindless sitcoms with their laugh tracks on TV in the emergency waiting room, and the eventual assurance from the doctor that the hemorrhage was old, not fresh blood.

The oncologist had told Kelly that she would be the doctor on call at cancer camp the following week and that it was perfectly fine for her to go in two days. This pleased Kelly endlessly and immediately lightened her spirits. At the same time, Lauren and Leslie would be away at the beach with extended family. Rob and I would stay home, available to her if any medical crisis arose.

Kelly knew we had an appointment on Tuesday of that week to go to C.H.O.P. to discuss "options" with the oncology team. While she had fun at camp, Rob and I desperately missed her at home, knowing she wouldn't be long for this world. It was nearly the saddest week of our lives.

It was torturous, but necessary playback. The year before, I had felt like I would throw up all week, having to tell Kelly what we learned, and to start the process of preparing her, and our family, for her death. Now, I replayed our conversations with Kelly after we picked her up from camp, and with her sisters after they returned from the beach. I replayed the weeks before our trip to Disney World, the dolphins, the airplane, the van ride home from the airport, the headache. Jesus had his *Via Dolorosa*, or "the way of suffering" en route to his death. This was ours.

I went through the motions of my daily life, but the lead-up to the first anniversary of her death was all I could focus on. I was *there*, reliving every bittersweet memory of our trip to Disney World in excruciating detail. In staff meetings, I would listen and contribute, but it was the procession of events from the year before that had my soul's undivided attention.

On Tuesday, September 20, the first anniversary of her death, I had planned a late afternoon walk to the cemetery with Tucker before Rob and the girls returned from school and we'd all go out to dinner as a family. I had dreaded this day and wanted to have some alone time with my own emotions before sharing them with everyone else. I pictured myself sitting on her grave with our dog, wondering if he'd sense her underneath the ground.

At 4:00 p.m., the time of her death, I leashed up Tucker, and we set out together. A ghost of a full moon was visible just above the houses to our left. We could've been there in five minutes if we'd cut through the neighbor's yards and the farmer's cornfield. Instead, we stayed on the asphalt.

As we entered the cemetery, I felt like a nursing mother hearing her baby cry, only it was a let-down of tears and not milk. Here was the place I could grieve, uninterrupted, and not worry about anyone seeing me.

We were just about to her grave when there was a flash of motion out of the corner of my eye. Suddenly, a dog shot out from behind a tombstone and lunged at Tucker's neck. The two tangled in a vicious swirl of growling and biting until a man in a far section of the cemetery over the hill gave a loud whistle and called his aggressive dog off mine. The skirmish lasted only 10 or 15 seconds, but my heart was pounding out of my chest, and Tucker was left with blood on the white swath of fur around his neck.

The man and his dog disappeared, but I wanted to scream at him at the top of my lungs for letting his dog off leash so that mine got injured, ruining my perfectly sad evening. Instead, my knees buckled, and I knelt on top of Kelly's grave. A few expletives escaped. Then I fell to my stomach and began to cry hard, beating the ground with my fists. *GOD, WHEN WILL THIS PAIN END?!*

Just like that it was loose—this monster with the power to crush anyone in its path. There is too much quietness in grief. It gets tired of slow dancing and wants to rumba.

Poor Tucker. The loop of his leash in my hand, I lay face down on the grave, crying loud, angry sobs.

Later that evening, the four of us went to dinner at the village family restaurant next to the cemetery. But we might as well have been on bad blind dates with each other. Emotions were logjammed. Conversation was stilted.

We laid flowers on her grave after dinner, then went home and dispersed into separate corners of the house. We could've lit a candle at home, group-hugged, and simply acknowledged, "This hasn't been easy, has it?" But I knew I would burst open and upset the girls. I wonder if everyone else felt that way, too.

I regret so much that neither Rob nor I could shepherd our daughters any better through this. The evening was a very sad blackout in my mind. It was like a star athlete coming home after losing a championship game, or a pianist after a humiliating memory lapse during a concert solo. There was simply nothing to be said that could make any of it feel any better.

The next morning, we officially entered Year Two. I suppose part of me thought that the first anniversary of her death was the last hurdle, and that we were now over the worst of it. But Year Two drives home the reality that what happened in Year One isn't going to change. Kelly's vacation away from us wasn't coming to an end, like maybe we thought it might. There was no heavenly payback or reward for all the suffering. It was just more of the same, setting in colder and harder.

CHAPTER ELEVEN

Making sense of a God who rips your heart out

Throw at him your grief, your anger, your doubt, your bitterness, your betrayal, your disappointment—
he can absorb them all.
— PHILIP YANCEY

In season two of *The Big Bang Theory* spin-off TV show, *Young Sheldon,* Sheldon's mother, Mary Cooper, tells her mother that she was making a casserole to bring over to friends who had lost their child. "I wanted to include a sympathy card," she explains. "So, I started to write, 'Your daughter's in a better place.' And I had to stop. Because how could that possibly be true? How could a better place be anywhere than at home safe with her family? She was just a little kid."

That's the soft-pedaled rub of a deeper issue that cracks open the hearts of suffering people everywhere. How do you make sense of a loving God who rips your heart out? Does tragedy just randomly happen in the natural world, or is it the will of God all along? And if it is the latter, how horribly cruel of a loving God, or so it seems.

Like most children in secure, loving families, I wasn't raised to expect bad things to happen. Though I had my fair share of childhood anxieties, many evenings after the dishes were done, my mother and father would play piano and harmonica together in the living room, making it seem as if we didn't have a care in the world. I do remember Dad telling me one time, "People will always disappoint. Don't put your trust in them, put it in God." What he didn't warn me about was the possibility that God might disappoint, too.

Our city congregation built a new church in the suburbs when I was six years old, the focal point of which was a sanctuary with a high ceiling and a steeple that towered over the front door and surrounding neighborhood. I was terrified of thunderstorms back then and would flee to my bed under a pile of quilts every time I saw a large mass of dark clouds approaching across the fields to the northwest. I had looked up the word *lightning* in our World Book Encyclopedia so many times to rehearse how to stay safe during storms, that the "L" volume automatically fell open to it.

So, I listened intently as Dad explained that the new church steeple was equipped with a metal rod that would attract lightning during a storm and send it straight down to the ground. I understood that this was a good thing—for the building to be *grounded*—which would prevent the church from catching fire. But I was perplexed as to why the builders would ever have wanted to *attract* lightning.

The brand-new sanctuary had magnificent acoustics. I would enter the cavernous space in the dark after children's choir practice and bounce a sung "ah" off its walls, then run to the lit hallway for safety, my heart pounding wildly, because I felt as if that lightning rod may also be inadvertently attracting spiritual power, and God himself may have answered in the echo.

That sanctuary became an enormous part of my spiritual formation. At home, I was taught faith principles in the warmth of a loving family. But the sanctuary was where I could envision God's bigness. The music was how I *felt* it. Undergirded by a powerful pipe organ and enhanced by the choir, the congregational worship reached deep into my soul, helping my spirit and faith soar to match the building's physical space and beyond.

It was a natural progression for me to take my affinity for music into college, where my faith deepened and I honed my skills toward certification in music education and music therapy. Years later, after I quit my professional job to raise children, and as churches had need of musicians, I flowed naturally in and out of paid and unpaid positions. Worship and the arts gradually mushroomed into a full-time vocation.

Over the years, in a variety of faith settings, I embraced the message that surrender, trust, and praise were the proper response to every difficulty in life, and that the best inherent rewards came when you put others' needs before your own. Missing in there were two key principles that no one really taught, and that would take me years to absorb and put into practice—*lament* and *self-care*.

I once worked with an atheist who said to me, a little tongue in cheek, "You Christians like to suffer, right? Isn't that what you do?" She hit a nerve, because I was born into a church community that valued service and humility. And when you're an empathetic soul raised and natured to care for others, it can feel self-indulgent to accept help when you're the one who desperately needs it. It can also be easy to overlook the hurting people in your own family. I sometimes made the mistake of assuming they should want to care for the whole world like I did just because they were my own flesh and blood.

In February of 1992, our family of five started attending a new church. On our first Sunday there, the congregation prayed *A Covenant Prayer in the Wesleyan Tradition*. We had gone through a heartbreaking church split six months before, which cost me my job, so the opening lines, booming with several hundred voices, cut me to the quick: *I am no longer my own, but thine. Put me to what thou wilt, rank me with whom thou wilt. Put me to doing, put me to suffering. Let me be employed by thee or laid aside for thee.*

The line, *put me to suffering*, rolled right over me.

With Kelly's diagnosis just four months later, lightning struck the steeple of my faith. I felt anything *but* grounded. Up until then, I thought I knew what prayer and faith were. I didn't know the extent to which fear and emotion could flood the brain's center of language so that only gasps, gulps, and guttural sounds, the most primal form of language, can be accessed. My entire body, in effect, *became my prayer.*

The Saturday afternoon when Kelly's neurosurgeon in Philadelphia came to her room to talk to our family about her upcoming surgery, he was straightforward, kid-friendly, and reassuring. But surgery on a tumor attached to the brain stem is perilously delicate work. One little nick in the wrong place, he told us, could leave her badly impaired. He didn't spare us worst-case scenarios. Rob and I were a crumbling façade, barely adjusted to the diagnosis, let alone the thought of our daughter's skull being cut into, the probability of cancer, and the possibility that she could be maimed or not survive. Our parents had rented a hotel room for us across the street from the hospital and urged us to take some time alone.

We couldn't get there fast enough. We threaded the hallways past bald children leashed to I.V. poles, waited for the elevator, endured an intrusive comment from a woman while riding down to the first floor, and booked it through the lobby to get out the door and across heavy traffic. We had barely registered at the desk, gone back up another elevator, fidgeted with the key, and pushed the door open before I tore back the covers on the bed and fell facedown onto the pillow.

For a long while, I was lost in the sound of my own deafening cries. Then, between gasps for air, I heard a strange sound I didn't recognize. I turned to look around to see what it was. It was my rock of a husband, bent forward on a loveseat near the bed, wailing with me.

The house of us shook violently for a while. These were the deepest, most agonizing prayers we'd ever prayed, testing the mettle of every fiber of our relationship with God. Finally, faces swollen and eyes bloodshot from strain, we looked up at each other through squinty eyes and blurred vision to assess the damage. "It hurts so much to think I can't shield her from all this, can't protect her or help her," Rob said, succumbing to a fresh spasm of tears.

Our minds latched onto Jesus in the Garden of Gethsemane the night before his death, asking for the cup to pass. We now understood something about the intensity of his prayers that caused him to sweat drops of blood, and of the trust and love that made surrender even possible.

In time, the hurricane moved through, and the air started to clear. We were intact, more grounded than we realized. In spite of a malignant pathology report, it was a positive outcome to the surgery three days later. After another 10 days in the hospital, a few days at home, and back to Philadelphia for six weeks of twice-daily radiation, Kelly's prognosis was hopeful for a five-year survival.

That fall, while Kelly's chemotherapy began at Hershey Medical Center, I accepted a youth choir position at our new church. I loved the teenagers, and it was refreshing to do something not hospital-related. In the spring, I was asked to take an interim position with the adult choir as well.

Five months later, right after I agreed to fill the position permanently, lightning struck again with Kelly's fateful MRI. Five emotionally devastating weeks later, she was gone.

Now, the real test of faith began. For Rob, the joyous and hopeful hymns and songs during church services became knives to his heart. The lyrics pointed to God's faithfulness, to eternal life, to hope—and now, to a seeming betrayal of his faith. One Sunday, the sermon text was the story of Jairus, who came to Jesus asking him to heal his seriously ill 12-year-old daughter. Jesus agreed, and on the way to see her, people intercepted their journey saying not to bother, that she had already died. But Jesus told them to have faith and assured them that she was only sleeping. Although they derided him for his remark, they were amazed when he got to her bedside, took her by the hand and said, *"Talitha koum!"* ("Little girl, I say to you, get up!") The little girl got up, and Jesus told them to give her something to eat.

This story poured salt into the wound for Rob and shattered his confidence in other scriptural promises. He wasn't jealous of Jairus. He just wanted some account in the New Testament to fit our scenario, to assure him that Jesus didn't *always* heal people, and that it wasn't a matter of how much faith you had. But if there are any such stories, they are absent from the Bible. He had never prayed harder for anything or anyone in his whole life. What now, he thought, was the point of praying? Heaven didn't seem to respond, or even to have much empathy.

For me, it was a little different. Songs took on piercingly deep meaning. In a Sunday morning worship service in the first year after Kelly's death, the choir was preparing to lead in a choral arrangement of a song about God's strength being made perfect in our weakness. I stood at the lectern to say a few words to introduce it and to ask the congregation to join us on the chorus. But as I lifted my arms to bring in the congregation, and their multiplied voices swelled in volume around me, I had to stop singing and bury my head in my hands for the rest of the chorus until I could recover. I loved them all for continuing to sing in spite of me, for corporately supporting and carrying me.

Within the next year, I was asked to start a praise band, adding to the church's traditional services one, then two, contemporary music worship services. It had become the popular norm in contemporary worship design all over the country to open services with a 10-minute set of upbeat praise songs. But that kind of music can be an abrasive call to worship for grieving people.

I read a statistic during those years suggesting that on any given Sunday, 50% of people in a congregation are grieving something. It sometimes felt wrong to me, as a worship planner, to insert the expected opening worship set of upbeat songs and hymns when half the congregation may have needed something much slower and more thoughtful.

Singer/songwriter Michael Card writes in *A Sacred Sorrow: Reaching Out to God in the Lost Language of Lament*, "We were created to live [with God] in a garden, and yet we awake every morning in the desert of a fallen world.... Bound by the personal sorrows and hurts we leave outside the door on a thousand Sundays, we are left to languish while those around us drink from a fountain that, to our eyes, looks dry.... Our best hope of finding our way back to true worship lies along the pathway of lament.... It provides the only trustworthy bridge to God across the deep seismic quaking of our lives."

I look back over some of the journals I wrote in the early years and regret how I rushed myself to praise, instead of allowing myself room to lament. Before I wrote a family Christmas letter 15 months after Kelly died, one friend cautioned me to be careful not to "uphold the myth" that you get over a death like this in a couple of years. She said it because she knew that I had difficulty during those first two years allowing myself the truth of my own feelings, especially around other people. Inside, I was an emotional basket case. Outside, I was a people pleaser who didn't want to impose on anyone or expose the shame of my endless inconsolability.

One time another friend caught me apologizing for and glossing over my feelings. "Lisa," she said firmly. "This isn't your *pet canary* that died." To grieve well through the years, I had to allow myself to linger longer and more honestly in the depths of sadness, and not to brush spiritual varnish over my pain.

In the journal we found in her bedside table drawer, Kelly wrote that she felt like she was a missionary for God's love. So of course, along with her stunning dream of eating with Jesus, this was the banner I carried. Why wouldn't I? It was the only truly comforting thing I had to hold onto. Still, to this day, it brings me tremendous hope and solace. It was also how I answered for myself the especially tricky question many bereaved parents ask of their child's death: *Was it God's will?* For me, there was no other explanation. Because if her death wasn't at least God's permissive will, whose was it? And how utterly devastating it would have been to think that there was nothing redeemable about such a horrible tragedy.

At the same time, it didn't seem to us, or to anyone around us, that the aggressive cancer in our daughter's brain was God's will. Otherwise, why would we have prayed so hard against it and given consent to such radical treatment to remove and restrain it? But to hold the view that our spiritually-attuned daughter was carrying around in her body—and succumbing to—a ravaging evil force, didn't make sense either. Was her death due just to the science of hormones, environment, and genetics? And then that begged the next question: *Why were God's hands tied to stop it?*

My sister asked me one day if I was angry at God. "No, I'm really not," I told her.

"But you're talking like you're angry with people," she said. "Isn't that just a way of redirecting your anger at God?"

During Kelly's 15-month illness, people came out of the woodwork and gave us all kinds of things—ceramic angels, patron saint bookmarks, toys, food, stuffed animals, books on healing cancer, clothing, arts and crafts, notes, flowers, trinkets, you name it. A few weeks after she died, I opened up the craft drawer in our kitchen and stared at over 20 brand new coloring books, each with an unopened box of crayons—all gifts from well-wishers during Kelly's illness. I could have donated them somewhere. But instead, it just hurt to look at them. In an impulsive moment, I grabbed a trash bag and angrily tossed them all into it.

As I was cinching the top with a tie, I felt a tender, but clear chastisement in my spirit: *Every box of crayons was given to you by someone whose heart was breaking for you, who didn't know how else to show it.* And then I sank to the floor and cried out of shame at how ungrateful I'd been and how confusing everything felt.

Maybe it was anger at God. I was certainly feeling frustrated and lost. But it was also a disillusionment that C.S.

Lewis aptly described in *A Grief Observed*: "Not that I am (I think) in much danger of ceasing to believe in God. The real danger is of coming to believe such dreadful things about him. The conclusion I dread is not, 'So there's no God after all,' but, 'So this is what God's really like. Deceive yourself no longer.'"

We were on a return flight from Wyoming two years after Kelly died, having taken a family trip with Rob's parents. We had postponed it from the year before because we were not emotionally at a place where we could enjoy it. There was a bit of turbulence over the Rocky Mountains. Rob and the girls were casually playing cards that jittered around on their dining trays, but I was white-knuckling it across the aisle. I shut my eyes, going in and out of prayer, taking shallower and shallower breaths, then spinning out into a swirl of fear and anxiety as I pictured our plane losing control and hurtling into a mountain.

What was happening? What had changed? Then a strong prayer rose up within me: *I don't trust you anymore to protect me.* If God hadn't spared Kelly, then why should I assume God would spare me or the rest of my family ever again? Furthermore, it seemed, prayer didn't necessarily make things better. In fact, it seemed to stir up dark forces. Why make life even more scary and miserable by praying about it?

It rings hollow for me when I hear someone imply that "answered prayers" mean things have gone the way they'd hoped, and that "blessings" are when something good happens—for example, "Praise God—my mother is in remission!" "All glory to God—our team won the championship!" In other words, *I feel happy, because my particular God is doing things the way I think they should be done.*

All that keeps us stuck in a very small, self-centered world. When God shakes that up by coming out of character (at least the one we've created for him), we become disillusioned. Are any of us less blessed when our teams don't win? When we can't conceive the child we long for? When we can barely make ends meet? When illness takes a turn for the worse, or when life is so raw and blindingly painful that our gentle, reverent prayers turn into primal screams and pounding fists?

Bishop Robert Barron tells this story: "There was this lady who spent a long time in a Catholic hospital while her husband was dying, going through months and months of agony. Finally, she goes outside and sees a statue of Mary. She starts picking up clots of dirt and throwing them at the statue in a rage. Security sees what's happening and starts to pull her back, but the hospital chaplain comes out and says, 'Don't stop her... she's praying.'"

Here was the power of transformation through suffering for me: to allow my tumultuous inner life to overflow in lament, to throw those clots of dirt, to surrender to the dance hold of the partner I didn't ask for—*then,* to proclaim words of faith from within that embrace, words like "Yet this I call to mind and therefore I have hope. Because of the Lord's great love, we are not consumed, for his compassions never fail" (Lamentations 3). These words follow a list of harrowing afflictions in the preceding verses, and I plunged them into the steep granite wall in front of me like a rock climber's anchor.

In the confusion of judgments, interpretations, and platitudes, thankfully there were friends and family who didn't clutter our hearts with any of these. They just dropped lifelines of hope and care when we needed them. Some organized memorials at her school. Some spoke words of hope and helped to stabilize us. Others helped us take deep breaths again. Many of their overtures came at what seemed like divinely appointed times, which only pointed to the reality that we weren't actually being abandoned, but rather cared for in heavenly ways.

Our friend Michelle showed up at our door on July 30, ten months after Kelly died, with a gallon jug of homemade tea brewed from the mint leaves in Kelly's memorial garden at the school. I was deeply touched. "How did you know it was her birthday?"

"It's her birthday?" she asked, incredulous. "Gosh, I didn't know. I just happened to be over at the garden, picked some leaves, and wanted to make you this tea."

Another time, my mother found a sweet picture she had taken of Kelly right before she was diagnosed. I had never seen it and wanted to frame it. When the framer got the picture off the shelf to ring up at the cash register, he said in broken English, "And who is this beautiful little girl?"

"My daughter," I said. "She passed away."

Very tenderly, he wrapped the frame and placed it in my hands and bowed his head slightly. "There is no cost for this today; it is my gift."

And then there was 10-year-old Cindy. One Sunday after the service, I lingered alone in the front church pew, relishing a chance to finally emote after a worship service that had raked me open. After the people had filed out and I had cleaned up all the music, I saw that the doors had closed in the back. I sat down in the front pew and released my pent-up emotion.

I didn't hear the door open, but I felt a presence behind me. I turned, and there she was, a child about the size of Kelly, with blonde hair and blue eyes just like hers, standing quietly in the back of the sanctuary, smiling at me, watching me intently. The resemblance was striking and a little eerie. I wiped my nose and said, "Well, hello, what's your name?"

"Cindy," she said. "Are you sad?"

"Yes, Cindy, I am. I have a daughter who died. I miss her very much."

"I know," she said. "My mom told me. I hope you feel better." I later learned that this extraordinarily sensitive child was also homesick for someone—to be reunited with her sister from whom, due to a legal complication, she had been separated since her adoption.

I don't know that it's possible to ever make sense of a God who rips your heart out. Some things we will never understand. But I believe the Spirit comes to us in a host of inexplicable and tender ways that help us begin to bear with serenity all that is, at first, unbearable. If we allow ourselves to trust the arms and the movement of grief, and stay long enough within its grasp, suffering will flow through and transform us.

When Jesus came to Kelly in her dream, he gave her a picture of extraordinary companionship. This companionship with God is all that really makes sense to me when everything else is completely unfathomable. That he would give me a customized, earthly version of this nearly two years later, in the form of an actor who portrayed *Jesus*, of all people, calls for a chapter unto itself.

CHAPTER TWELVE

When God enters our pain

*Suffering is unbearable if you aren't certain
that God is for you and with you.*
—— TIM KELLER

About a month before the first anniversary of Kelly's
death, on an extended family vacation in a distant state,
I picked up a local entertainment magazine and was intrigued to read a glowing review of an actor named Daniel
Dupree,* who was portraying Jesus in a limited run at a
nearby theater. I was intensely curious to read about his
one-man show and regretted that we wouldn't be in town
for the remaining performance dates.

I was fascinated by the meticulous research and care
he'd taken to use only the book of Matthew as his script
and to historically authenticate his costume, hair, and
makeup. And I was moved by quotes from locals who

---

* Name has been changed to protect privacy.

knew him personally, vouching for what a wonderful person he was.

There had been a phone number at the end of the article to call for bookings, so when we got home, I approached the leadership at church to ask what they would think about engaging him for a weekend of performances. They were intrigued. They gave me the green light to move forward with plans.

I placed a call, expecting to speak with Daniel's agent. I was caught off-guard when he picked up the phone himself. I asked him if he could come in April (he could), and if he'd like me to book him at a few more venues in order to make his trip more worthwhile (he would be so grateful). Eventually we agreed on a schedule when he'd be in Lancaster for five days, doing six presentations.

During my childhood, my parents had occasionally hosted out-of-town guests of our church for extended periods of time, so it felt perfectly natural for me to ask him whether he'd like to stay with us while he was in town. "But I completely understand if you'd prefer a hotel. I'm guessing you'd appreciate the privacy."

"Actually, I prefer to stay in homes, if possible," he said. "I find hotels to be pretty lonely."

While Daniel had agreed to perform for freewill offerings, there wasn't a line item in our church budget for lodging, so Rob and I decided we would pick up the tab ourselves. Daniel's decision to stay with us made it a whole lot easier financially. "I need to let you know, though, that we have a dog, and you'd be sleeping in our guest room, which was the room of our youngest daughter, who passed away. If that's uncomfortable at all for you—"

"I love dogs, and I'd be honored to stay in her room," he said. "I once stayed in a kid's car bed. It was great fun." By this, our third phone call, I had warmed to this creative, humble, and articulate soul. I couldn't wait to meet him.

For weeks our family worked at wrapping our minds around the idea of "Jesus" coming to live with us. I reminded us all, including myself, that he was an actor, a real person. While it was certainly part of my job to create worshipful, dramatic arts experiences for people at church, I had also been in heavy grief for the last 15 months. Subconsciously, maybe I was really yearning for something much deeper.

This would be the first time anyone else had slept in Kelly's room. The day before his arrival, I looked at her twin bed covered with a stained, floral comforter. *Not suitable for an adult man.* So, I went out and bought another one.

When Rob got home from work that evening, he went upstairs to change and passed by Kelly's bedroom. Agitated, he came downstairs. "What did you pay for that new bedspread?"

"I'm not having a grown man sleep in a bed with girly flowers and permanent stains."

"He's going to be here for less than a week. Why would you buy a new spread just for that?"

"Because I'm thinking he'll not be the last guest we'll ever have."

He was clearly upset. What was going on? Finally, he sat down at the kitchen table, put his head in his hands, and rubbed his forehead for a moment. His next words were softer, revealing the real heart of the matter. "I'm not ready for a new bedspread in her room."

I melted when I remembered how upset Lauren was when I shut Kelly's bedroom door at night. Or how furious I was, months before, when I opened the drawer in our bathroom and saw that the sliver of blue soap had been thrown out. "What's the big deal?" Rob said when I burst into tears. "It's just an old bar of soap."

"It's the soap Kelly took to camp!" I'd cried. "I get it out sometimes just to smell it, to feel close to her."

He had been truly sorry, and now it was my turn to understand. "I still have her bedspread in the closet upstairs," I said. "I'll put it back on the bed after he leaves."

The next afternoon, Daniel pulled into our driveway in a white Jeep Wrangler with a black convertible top. He slid out of it, a spry, blond, beachy-looking guy resembling nothing in his promo photos of Jesus or the image I'd built up in my head about him.

I helped him carry his luggage upstairs to Kelly's room. "You can hang your things in here," I told him, opening the bi-fold door of her closet. There were still a few items of her clothing hanging to one side, and some of her stuffed animals, toys, and books stored on the top shelf.

But I'd cleared plenty of space. "The bathroom's right across the hall, towels are on the counter. Take your time to rest or freshen up. When you're ready to come down, I've got tea and cookies."

He came back down within just a few minutes and watched me pour the tea. "How long ago did your daughter pass away?"

"A year and a half. Still feels pretty fresh."

"I'd imagine so." He took the mug I handed him and spooned honey into it. "Was that your daughter's teddy bear on the top shelf in the closet?"

I was touched that he had noticed. It was pink and worn, washed clean after a year of being pressed against our hearts, and now zipped up in a clear vinyl storage bag to preserve it forever. *But for what*, I suddenly thought, with a twinge of regret.

"I hope you don't mind my asking."

"No, not at all."

"I just felt like he needed to breathe."

I paused, holding the plate of cookies. "You're probably right," I said. "Here, please help yourself."

We talked for over two hours before Rob came home, connecting quickly and deeply about life, faith, grief, and the arts.

Later, while Rob was getting to know our new guest, I went upstairs and took the bear out of storage and set him on the bureau. Daniel's words were an invitation. I wanted to accept.

That night at dinner he gushed over the meal, then sent our family into uncontrollable fits of laughter as he regaled us with his imitation of a flight attendant from one of his recent trips.

When he asked me before bed if we happened to have any Ovaltine (we actually *did*), I knew he was one of my tribe. I was the only one in the family who liked it, and I was happy to have someone to enjoy it with.

The next morning I drove him to a private high school for his first presentation, an assembly of about 900 students. I sat way in the back, watching the curtain open on what looked like a low-level, tan-colored rock formation in the desert. A hush fell over the audience when suddenly it moved, and the hooded face of Jesus emerged from the formation, lifting slowly to gaze at the audience.

"What did you go out into the wilderness to see?" he said. "A reed swayed by the wind? If not, what did you go out to see? A man dressed in fine clothes? No, those who wear fine clothes are in kings' palaces."

I watched him rise from the rock formation, which was really his body in a heap in his muslin robe, then move slowly across the stage as he spoke, descending the stairs and moving through the aisles. I saw him place his mantle around the neck of a napping student, gently teasing him awake, then take the hand of another student and lead him up to the stage to wash his feet, like Jesus had done to his disciples in biblical times.

He had the grace and unnerving quality of Jesus to challenge, to disturb the status quo, to lock eyes with a student and say, "You are the salt of the earth. But if the salt loses its saltiness, how can it be made salty again?" and then to another, "You are the light of the world. A town built on a hill cannot be hidden. Neither do people light a lamp and put it under a bowl. Instead, they put it on its stand, and it gives light to everyone in the house. In the same way, let your light shine before others."

I was astounded. His transformation was so profound, I simply did not recognize the man who had sat at dinner with us the night before. (He told me later that he would often go into the lobby after performances to hear what people were saying—and was *never* recognized.)

I took him to a restaurant afterward for lunch, then to our church to see the layout for his performance the following night. He gestured toward the piano. "You told me you write music. I would love if you'd play me something you've written."

I hadn't written anything since Kelly got sick. I wasn't sure I ever wanted to again. But by now I was so completely comfortable around Daniel that I didn't argue. I slid onto the bench and thought for moment. "This is something I wrote a very long time ago." I searched a little to remember the beginning, but then it began to flow—a rendering of the words of Jesus in John 15.

"That's one of the most beautiful songs I've ever heard," he said softly. "Please play and sing some more." I wasn't used to this kind of audience. I was disarmed and deeply moved by his receptivity and attentiveness to every lyric and nuance of the music.

Later, we joined the family for dinner and continued to talk well into the evening. Daniel explained to me that he always made fresh communion bread (never bought) before every performance, had brought his own ingredients, and asked me if I would mind if he used our kitchen in the morning. I put out a rolling pin and pans and gladly turned it over to him while I went to a meeting at church.

When I returned later that Saturday morning, I found him happily kneading dough. Soon he had shaped the dough into loaves, covered them with tea towels, and cleaned up every last trace of flour. "Lisa, would you mind putting these into the oven for me after they rise? Rob wants to take me out for a drive."

Rob drove Daniel deep into the heart of Amish country, far from the tourist attractions. He got to appreciate the beauty of Daniel's insightful questions and observations, and it amused him when Daniel shyly slid down in his seat so as not to be seen gawking at the occasional horse and buggy. Rob pulled over at one point, turned off the ignition, and said, "C'mon, let's get out. I want you to hear what quiet sounds like."

They stood together in silence, surveying immaculate fields set against an expansive gray sky. A lone Amishman way in the distance stood on a manual plow behind a team of mules, patiently tilling the rich dark soil for the spring planting. "Listen to the wind," Rob said, closing his eyes and letting the northwest breeze caress his face.

"This is genuine soul food," Daniel whispered. They stood there for a long while until the cold set into their bones and made them retreat back to the car.

When they got home, the aroma of baking bread filled the house. I was glad to see them both, surprised at how natural it felt to have Daniel in our home.

That night and the next morning during three services, Daniel mesmerized our church with his portrayal. At one of his presentations, a three-year-old girl whispered to her mother, asking her to help her write something, then couldn't help herself in the middle of the performance. She slipped out of her seat and raced down the aisle to hand it to Jesus. Right in the middle of a mournful soliloquy before the part in the narrative about the crucifixion, "My soul is very sorrowful, even unto death," she burst onto the platform to hand him her note. Caught completely off-guard by her, Daniel stopped and read *I love you* on the note, then barely missed a beat as he smiled and hugged her, altering his text. "But you have made my heart glad!"

That's what it was like with him in our home, especially for me—initiative, response, surprise, blessing—over and over. Was this how Kelly felt in her dream of eating with Jesus at a table for two—so deeply and utterly filled with his presence?

The boulders in my soul were beginning to lighten.

That afternoon, Daniel wanted to rest before his evening performance while Rob watched a football game. It was a cold day, and Rob had built a fire and invited him to conk out there in the family room with him. He did, and nestled into the L-shaped couch in the family room, exactly where Kelly would lie, and slept for a couple of hours.

He was filling, awakening, and revitalizing the grief-soaked spaces in our lives—her bedroom, her place on the couch, her place at the table, our faith, our church, our sense of humor. He fed and let Tucker out, he washed dishes, he helped out around the house. He had moved in and blended in like family. He had baked bread, but he was filling us with the Bread of Life.

On his last night with us, a school night, Rob and the girls turned in early, and Daniel and I talked for a while longer at the kitchen table. Over mugs of hot Ovaltine, I gently inquired about the hint of sadness I had noticed in his eyes, and he revealed some of the tender, broken, and lonely places in his own heart. He'd been good for us, but our family had also been good for him.

"I've got a long drive tomorrow," he said finally. "I'd better turn in."

We stood and embraced. I kissed his cheek, trying to drink in the gift of him as much as possible before he left.

The next morning I watched his Jeep round the bend on our street and disappear from view. And then I promptly went into the front room and wept. I felt like I was inhabiting the final scene drawn by the boy in *The Little Prince* when he said: "This is to me, the loveliest and saddest landscape in the world…. It is here that the little prince appeared on Earth, and disappeared."

For weeks after he left, my heart would shred a little bit whenever I saw another white Jeep Wrangler like his on the road. But Kelly's teddy bear never went back into storage after that, and—with Rob's blessing—the new bedspread stayed on her bed. For the last couple of years, I had been a dry riverbed with my music, but I started to compose again.

Over the next years, we would host Daniel two more times for different historical portrayals. We've remained friends to this day as his career has taken him to Hollywood and off-Broadway. But it was his first visit that helped me understand how God comes to us in our suffering—in ways we don't expect, through strangers who are not yet friends, and by deeply inhabiting with us the places where it hurts the most.

CHAPTER THIRTEEN

Grieving alone, grieving together

When you cry, I cry, and when you hurt, I hurt.
— Nicholas Sparks

There have been countless moments in our marriage when either Rob or I will be triggered to tears and have to stop and let a wave of grief move through, while the other gently holds vigil until it passes. But it hasn't always been that way.

In the beginning, because we were on the same timeline with events, I expected that our family would grieve in unison. But each of us had a unique relationship with Kelly, and thoughts triggering waves of grief were as out of phase with each other as they could possibly be.

One afternoon, weeks after Daniel had gone, I sat down at the piano and wrote my first song since Kelly died. That night after dinner, I said to Rob, "Come into the living room. I want to play you something." He'd always been highly supportive of my music, and I really wanted to share this song with him.

He sat down beside the piano, and I said, "This is about Kelly's dream, if I can get through it." I faltered the first time I started, then started again, then got choked up at one point, but kept going.

When I was done, he was quiet for a minute, then said, "It seems like it took you a long time to get to the point. Do you need all that in the beginning?"

I had been a Japanese pearl diver who had not been in the water or had a catch for a long time. I had spent all day diving to find this one pearl, and he was already criticizing it. "*This* is the first thing you have to say to me? I write a song about our daughter, my first song in two years, and this is all you can say?"

"I just thought it meandered at the beginning—"

"I just got it down on the page! I'm not ready yet to hone it to perfection!"

I dissolved into tears and fled the room. He came to me up in the bedroom and said how sorry he was. But there was no consoling me.

The next morning before he left for work, he said again how sorry he was. But he had clipped the bud of my creativity, and I had no confidence I would ever get it back. Later that evening before dinner, he again said how sorry he was, but I couldn't stop hurting about it, and now his apologies were just pouring salt into a very complex wound.

That weekend, we attended one of Lauren's night soccer games. After it was over, we were walking through a large, dimly lit grassy field to get to our car and got separated when someone stopped him to ask a question. When he ended his conversation, he ran to catch up to me. I still didn't want to be around him, so I walked faster.

Finally, he caught me by the arm and said, "Lisa, *stop.*" There, in the uncomplimentary pallor of the stadium light towers, he turned to face me and said, "I am so, so, so sorry for hurting you. You're a great composer, we both know that. Please...will you *please* forgive me?"

This time I melted. "The beginning of the song did meander too much. I just wasn't ready to hear it then."

"But it was insensitive of me. Can we please let this go now?" There was no point in delving any deeper than that at the time. We had gone through the same experience of losing our daughter, but we were still very different people with different triggers.

It wasn't just our immediate family that was out of sync with each other. Rob's parents took Lauren to another one of her traveling soccer games in Philadelphia, and the three of them were having dinner together afterward at a nearby restaurant. His mother was chatting away about something when suddenly his father put his head in his hands and burst into tears. He had been triggered by their proximity to Children's Hospital of Philadelphia and was overcome with memories.

At the end of the first school year after Kelly's death, I made a drawing of the girls in graduation caps and gowns to congratulate them on having completed another year. On Lauren's cap I wrote "10th grade," on Leslie's, "7th grade," and then I couldn't bear to leave Kelly out. So, I drew her in a little gown with "Earth" on her cap. It had felt satisfying to me to tape it to the kitchen door leading to the garage, but when Rob got home and saw it, it upset him so much I took it down.

Kelly's birthday and the anniversary of her death were now as significant to us as other birthdays and holidays on the family calendar. The four of us faithfully marked those days together, but they were often emotionally awkward, and we just wanted to get through them. And as creative as we all are, we never managed, in those early years, to come up with a way to be more proactive about them.

Fast forwarding a little to a summer morning when both girls were home from college, I had an agenda of things I wanted them to do around the house, and I scolded them for having gone out to breakfast together. "Why *this* morning?" I asked, irritated.

They looked at each other, incredulous and a little wounded. "Because it's *Kelly's birthday*," Lauren said quietly. I'm sure my face turned crimson with shame. I hadn't forgotten it was the day, I just never expected them to take the initiative on their own to do something without us.

It's commonly thought to be true that after the death of a child, parents are 75-90% more likely to divorce than if their child had lived. For a while, those statistics terrified me. What was going to happen that we didn't know about that would tear us apart even further?

I've since learned that those statistics are misleading. What is true is that a child's death acts, instead, "to polarize the existing factors found in the marriage; hence, some marriages get worse, some get better, some just maintain, and some actually do end in divorce."

Our marriage has been challenged over the years in some exceedingly hard ways. We've had enough humility to seek help when we've needed it, apologize after we've been defensive, and to pray together. But grief of this magnitude is a special challenge. Family members are driven out onto separate islands, and you don't have enough strength, or experience rowing in such turbulent waters, to get to one another.

There are rare moments when synchronicity happens, and you don't feel so isolated in your pain. One Saturday night in September of 1995, two years into our grief, the girls were out with friends, and Rob and I had finished dinner and decided to turn on the TV. Back then, we didn't have a remote with a guide to surf channels. We just turned our set on and there he was—a cardiac surgeon conflicted about transplanting a new heart into the drunk driver who had killed his five children. The children and their mother had been in a car on their way to go sledding. The story snagged our attention. We weren't doctors, and we hadn't lost five children. But we knew something about his pain.

Since the accident, the surgeon had become estranged from his wife. At the same time, in the children's wing of the hospital, his artist wife was working on a sculpture that would stand as a memorial to their children.

We eventually figured out that the show was called *Touched by an Angel,* and we watched intently as the angel characters gently urged the husband and wife to move toward forgiveness with the driver and reconciliation with each other. At the end, after the husband successfully completed the surgery, one of the angels led him to another part of the hospital to see the sculpture his wife had been crafting. As he entered the room, the camera zoomed in on his wife's face, then the sculpture—a bronze statue of five children in a sled, faces bright with laughter, scarves flying in the wind.

I was seated on a swivel chair next to the window, and Rob was behind me on the couch. Neither of us like crying during a movie in the presence of the other, and if we do, we try to hide it. But the moment when the statue was revealed was so utterly overwhelming for me that I couldn't help myself. I immediately burst into sobs, gasped for breath, folded my head into my arms, and just wailed.

I swiveled my chair around to go get a box of Kleenex, then saw that Rob, also, was helplessly sobbing. "That statue is your book," he choked out. The awkward barrier between us had come crashing down, and for a precious moment in time, we were in complete synchronicity.

After that, we were more gracious to each other in our grieving process. We seemed to more instinctively understand that grief would ebb and flow for each other at will, and that it was okay to just let it take the lead.

I cannot stress enough how awkward relational dynamics can be across the board in the beginning. Not only do family relationships change—friendships do, too. Suddenly the balance of give-and-take is lopsided as the bereaved person no longer has the energy to reach out in the way they once did, or they need emotional support in ways others aren't sensitive enough to know, or fully equipped enough to give.

We are all such different personalities with varying life experiences and expectations. Introverts hold in their feelings, while extroverts are forthcoming. Some are thinking types, while others are feeling types. Some are closer to the deceased than others and emote more easily. Some are deeply sensitive, while others are more pragmatic. Some pray for you in the quiet of their hearts, while others make more of a splash when they do something for you.

I've learned that it's all okay, that if one grandparent isn't sobbing over her plate at dinner, it doesn't mean she cares any less than the one who is. Or if, as happened to a colleague of mine, the receptionist whites out your child's name on the church membership Rolodex the day after they're killed in an accident, it doesn't mean they don't have their compassionate reasons.

Grieving people do well not to make assumptions about the level of compassion others have or don't have, or to compare levels and types of supportiveness. While some support may be especially helpful, and some unintentionally wounding, it's more helpful to trust that it all comes from a place of love.

It's also important to understand that support doesn't always come from where you expect it, or in the manner you think it should. It will come, I promise, when and from whom you truly need it.

CHAPTER FOURTEEN

The third and fourth years

For a seed to achieve its greatest expression,
it must come completely undone.
To someone who doesn't understand growth,
it would look like complete destruction.
— CYNTHIA OCCELLI

The summer before our third Christmas without Kelly, I was in the family room, sitting on the floor with stacks of sheet music and CDs. For church music directors, summer is the time of year when you receive the newest choral releases from publishers, and you plan ahead for choirs and music teams.

I was in a stable place, or so I thought—until I picked up one octavo called, "I Miss You Most at Christmastime" by Craig Courtney. I was immediately moved by the dedication: *Written in memory of the composer's son, Adam.* I popped in the CD.

A half hour later, after pushing the replay button 10 times in a row and positively drained and swollen from crying, I got up off the floor and sat in a chair for a while. *There is no way on earth I could ever do this piece with my choir,* I thought.

But tears are wordless prayers, and heaven was eavesdropping. *Why not?* came an instantaneous reply in my spirit. *Other people are hurting, too.*

That simple response changed my mood entirely. Five months later, my colleague Pastor David Woolverton and I completed a script shaped around Courtney's anthem. We were taking a risk for a Christmas production by shunning normal holiday production scenery—using, instead, a beautifully crafted and painted Styrofoam *tombstone*, of all things, as the focal point. Would this fly with people? Didn't they want only to be cheered up at holiday time? Our church was a place of excitement and burgeoning growth. This had the potential to give me a bad performance review. But the words kept compelling me: *Other people are hurting, too.*

This time I didn't have to get in my car and scream before leaving for planning meetings. I was listening to my grief (and the Holy Spirit) tell me what it wanted from me.

Every Christmas, a generous woman from the church would treat the staff of 15 or so to a festive lunch at a nice restaurant. It was never an ideal time for me, with the increased demands on the worship and music department at that time of year. But I appreciated her generosity, and getting away for an afternoon of fun with my colleagues was always the break I didn't know I needed.

The first and second Christmases after Kelly's death, I had dutifully attended and tried to smile. But this third Christmas, however, I woke up feeling like crying, and all morning at work didn't make it any better. The thought of forcing cheerfulness at a Christmas lunch didn't feel like a gift.

By now, two years into my grief, I was starting to honor myself and listen more carefully to my body. We were due at the restaurant in 25 minutes. When I pulled out of the church parking lot to turn right to go to the restaurant, I found myself turning left, instead—to go home.

It was entirely uncharacteristic behavior of me to call no one to let them know I wouldn't be coming, or even to break rank and risk hurting the generous giver's feelings. But this was emotional space I desperately needed. At home, I could freely release the built-up emotion. Surprisingly, no one called to see where I was. And not a word was mentioned about it. It was the most freeing day, and an important realization in my journey. You *have* to protect the moments you need. No one else is going to do it.

On a cold, overcast December morning two weeks later, the choir, actors, and dancers presented David's and my musical play for three consecutive services. Instead of clapping at the end of the performance, there were sniffles throughout the sanctuary. Tissues came out of pockets and purses. For one morning, the pressure valve had been taken off of Christmas, and people were given space to acknowledge the grief in their own hearts. We had created a sanctuary from all the pressure, a place to acknowledge the pain, freedom to express that life is often sad and painful. Most stunningly, over and over again we heard, "This is the best Christmas musical we've ever seen."

Before anyone contacts me to ask where they can get a copy of our script, I need to honestly tell you that we have lost it. Furthermore, we don't have the rights to package or market and sell the choir's anthems that were sung that morning, nor do I remember any of them other than the one piece that started the whole process. The production seemed to have been given to us for a moment in time for a particular people at a particular place. And that's where it will stay.

What's more important to remember is that *you* should listen to grief's instructions to you for your place and circumstances. It will invite you out onto the floor, and if you're soft and pliable and willing to be led, it will heal not only you, but maybe a whole lot of other people, too.

Life wasn't all sad, nor conscious working through grief. The fall before that Christmas program, Lauren's senior year, we were steeped in an exciting college search process with her and made several trips to art schools. She was already a skilled illustrator and one of the fastest runners on her soccer team. Her classmates had voted her homecoming queen, and she was a featured cello soloist in her final spring orchestra concert.

At graduation, she picked up multiple awards, and the newspaper did a senior spotlight on her. You know the kind of feature story, exploited all the time on reality TV shows where they highlight people who have triumphed over personal tragedy. Like most parents, we got caught up with her trajectory as well and were enormously proud of her. Certainly, she was doing well. We had no reason to believe otherwise.

But we should've paid closer attention. One night during her senior year, I found her sitting on the floor in her room with a large scissors, making jagged cuts into the beautiful new ivory silk orchestra blouse I had just bought her. I reacted quickly and chided her for willfully destroying it.

I should've taken a deep breath instead and thanked God she wasn't cutting her arms. High school is hard enough with all its academic and social pressures, let alone managing the illness and death of your sister. Seven-and-a-half years older than Kelly, Lauren sometimes seemed to me to have more of a maternal relationship with her than a sibling would normally have. I think I underestimated the depth of her grief. Teenagers who aren't dealing with the death of an immediate family member have hard lives, too. But our family was in complex emotional waters.

As an adult, she reflected back on that period: "All I received from people," she said, "was constant positive reinforcement for being strong and happy, doing well at school, appearing like I was in good spirits, excelling at sports, music, art, and academics. I thought to myself, *This is what people like. They want to see that you're the vibrant contrast to the dead one.* They think you're in a hole, and they want you to be out of it. Most teenagers feel they're invincible. But all I was thinking about was how mortal we all are, and what the probability was that I would die, too, from a brain tumor. I thought about dying all the time."

As I think back on her cutting that blouse, and the hole she punched another time in her closet wall, I understand far more now than I'm sure I did then. Sometimes your children are just too close to your nose to really see them. Distance vision is much more powerful.

We had hoped she'd pick a school relatively nearby, but it was Ringling School of Art and Design in Sarasota, Florida, that finally won her acceptance. Ringling had connections with Disney, and at the time, she thought she wanted to illustrate for them. It seemed like a positive place to form career connections. But we look back on that decision and wonder if we should have encouraged her to attend college closer to home. She made the decision only two years into our family grief. We feel like, had the school not been so far away, we could've been more supportive. *Or was she picking Florida to feel closer to our last week with Kelly?*

When we dropped her off at Ringling that hot, humid August, I was a mess inside. I tried to be cheerful as we hugged her goodbye under the palm trees. But Rob and I both cried driving out of the campus parking lot. She admitted, much later, that she did, too, going back that day to her dorm room.

At a choir rehearsal after we got home, one of the women noticed my sadness and came up to me afterward to put a firm hand on my shoulder. "Lisa," she said, her eyes penetrating mine. "Lauren is going to *come back.*"

It was tough for me to sort through the layers of loss.

By this point, Leslie had advanced to higher levels in gymnastics. I would pick her up from school at 2:30 p.m., hand her half an apple with a big mound of peanut butter and raisins stuffed into the cored-out center, and she'd munch it down during the five-minute drive to the gym. We'd pick her up again four hours later. She'd microwave her dinner, and then she'd head straight up to her room for homework. Sometimes I felt like the gymnastics community set the rules of her life, became her family, and was raising her. I hadn't wanted to adopt her out like that, but the sports machine had taken a strong hold when we weren't looking.

Just before Thanksgiving, after the fourth anniversary of Kelly's death, I put together a service for people feeling blue about the holidays. I stood up to speak to them at the end, and as I did, I realized, *I'm starting to feel better. I can breathe again.* I had been under water for four years and hadn't comprehended just how deeply, until I finally came up for air.

Helping other people was part of that healing.

CHAPTER FIFTEEN

Breathing again

My comfort in my suffering is this:
Your promise preserves my life.
— PSALM 119:50

I had attended a writer's conference and started the slow submission process for my first book, *A Table for Two*. Disappointing rejections trickled in. One publisher expressed interest, asked to keep my manuscript for an extra two months, then finally decided a book about a child who dies just wasn't going to sell.

Eventually a good friend suggested a local publisher, whose books she enjoyed reading and who she thought might be a good fit for mine. I submitted my manuscript, the editor liked what she read, and they agreed to publish my book. But an unforeseen issue with their company delayed it another year.

Altogether, it was nearly five years after Kelly's death till the first box of published books arrived at my doorstep. I knew the excitement of seeing my music in print. But this was more emotional. I thumbed through the book and checked it from head to toe like a newborn baby.

The delay in publication turned out to be helpful. I needed distance and objectivity before talking to crowds about it. The book signings were enjoyable, as was a TV interview. But then I got a call from a newspaper reporter saying that they'd like to do a story on me.

After my interview, the photographer stood me beside a big tree and asked me to hold my book up and smile. It didn't feel natural. "This is a book about my daughter's death," I explained. "It doesn't seem like I should look *happy*."

"Oh, no, you should definitely smile!" he insisted. So there I stood, holding my book up and grinning like it was a trophy rather than my broken heart spilled out all over its pages. The picture and article landed on the front page of the newspaper. Suddenly, what had been a very private and cathartic outpouring was thrust into public space.

Letters began to trickle in, several a day. I was deeply touched that people were so moved by the book. It's what I wanted, for Kelly's mission to be fulfilled. But like they had done all during her illness, dark forces slithered around in the shadows.

The first negative letter came with no return address or signature, from someone who claimed to know me in high school, saying I was only out for my own selfish gain. The second was a sketchily addressed envelope with no house number and an incorrect zip code. Inside, the message was formatted like a ransom note, with cut and pasted words from a magazine: "What kind of animal in the zoo exploits its own children for its own gain?" And then written in chiller scrawl: "A. Bair."

"Who are these people?" I cried over the phone to Pastor David.

"Go to your kitchen sink, light a match, and burn these two letters," he said. "Listen to the people in the other letters and to what they're saying."

It wasn't easy to do. Maybe, I thought, I needed the letters for evidence to give to the police in case someone was stalking me. Worse yet, *maybe these people were right about me*. Then I fell into a really dark emotional hole. But I did what David said. I struck a match in my sink and watched the ill-intentioned letters turn to smoldering ashes, even if I couldn't stop thinking about what was in them.

The newspaper publicity about the book opened the door to many other grieving families and speaking engagements. I exchanged letters with grieving mothers in other states, visited local homes on occasion, and spoke to groups of women, as well as bereaved parents. A *Guideposts* story about Kelly's table for two was published about the same time, and I was deeply touched when someone told me they were vacationing in Colorado and actually heard Kelly's dream featured in a sermon while visiting a church there.

Bereaved people find all kinds of creative ways to keep going, and these were mine—to embrace writing and speaking in the dance with grief. It wasn't that I chose them like costumes off a rack for a performance; it was rather that grief moved me in a direction that was completely right and natural for me. We do little things that make us feel better (like smell soap and get tattoos), and we do big things like create symphonies, write books, start foundations, and dedicate trees. Grief *compels* us. It is its own kind of music, the beat of a particular drummer, and we do well to dance to it.

Kelly's cancer buddy, Chris, had featured prominently in *A Table for Two*. The two of them had similar brain surgeries at C.H.O.P. just a day apart. They started radiation exactly the same day. His mother and I held onto each other for support every day for the whole summer in radiation clinic for 60 treatments, and saw each other regularly in chemo clinics. Their family was devastated when Kelly died. But in the years following, we were really happy that Chris was doing so well—until, suddenly, he wasn't. Just months after my book was published, we received word that Chris had passed.

Rob and the girls and I traveled to Philadelphia to attend his service. We walked into a large church with heavy, dark wood trim and sat in a pew not too far from the front. Chris, by now a 14-year-old, lay in an open casket at the front of the church. A woman wearing a black uniform with a white apron stood near his head. His father was their church's pastor, and after people had filled in the pews, we were stunned when he stepped into the pulpit.

He leaned into the microphone as a woman helped him slip an outstretched arm into the sleeve of his robe, singing in a strong voice, "Sometimes I cry..."

The congregation sang back to him, "Sometimes I cry..."

His voice grew more powerful. "Sometimes I sing!"

The power in their voices did, too. "Sometimes I sing!"

"But Jesus will help me!"

"Jesus will help me!"

And we were instantly swept up in our first African-American Homegoing, a powerful mixture of community lament and call-and-response rejoicing like we'd never experienced before. The service lasted three hours. The trip to the cemetery lasted another hour. After the interment, when I was finally able to make my way to Chris's mother, she clutched me tightly and wouldn't let go. We wept for a long moment on each other's shoulders, until a funeral director tapped me on the arm and said, "We need to keep moving here," and pulled us apart.

As I look back on that funeral director's action (which hurt me deeply, I will admit, not to mention how insensitive it was to Chris's mother), I realize moments like that typify so much of the grieving process: The alarm clock goes off in the middle of a good dream you're having about your loved one. Or you're having a deep conversation with someone at church and another person comes up to you and says, "I don't want to interrupt; I have just a quick question." Or someone asks how you are, and their cell phone rings and they take the call.

Grief is not an interrupter—it's a friend with all the time in the world. When it invites you to come away for the weekend, *go*.

That fall, Leslie received the second homecoming queen crown in the family. For a few years now, she had been fierce competition in the boys' gym, on the wall with the record for the most timed push-ups in a minute in the whole school—72. The Phys. Ed. instructor would pass her in the hall every so often and tell her that some boy had bested her record; would she like to try to better the new one?

Now we were immersed in a different kind of college search—schools with Division 1 gymnastics teams. Leslie had recruiting trips scheduled at five of them. We went with her to the University of New Hampshire, where her gymnast friend Katie competed, and she was set to make her next trip to Utah when a Penn State recruiter happened to stop by the gym to see another one of her teammates. That friend hadn't recovered fully from a back injury, and the recruiter spotted Leslie and invited her to come to the campus.

It was a heady experience going with her on that recruiting trip, mixing it up with coaches and gymnasts, and getting to meet the legendary Joe Paterno outside Beaver

Stadium, where he signed a football for her on the eve of his 300th win.

Soon after we returned home, the gymnastics coach called and made an offer, saying he would give her 24 hours to decide whether to accept.

Leslie promptly burst into tears.

She was not one to shop quickly for anything, and she had been looking forward to her other trips. Penn State felt too close to home, too familiar. Now the pressure was on.

Her local gymnastics coach couldn't believe she was wavering about her decision. "Penn State has a *fantastic* program!" he said. "Take the deal!"

She did, and the three of us had an informal signing party on the back porch, toasting her with flute glasses filled with sparkling cider. This decision felt easier to us than Lauren's. Leslie would be only a two-hour drive away, and we would be able to attend her home meets.

As Les finished her senior year, and I kept working at the church and taking occasional speaking engagements, my publisher asked me if I would consider writing a book of meditations for grieving parents. I agreed, and wrote a third of the book before the brakes inside me clamped down for dear life. I emailed my editor. "I'm so, so sorry. I just can't keep going with this book. Not right now."

Grief was calling me out onto the floor again—only this time it didn't want to slow dance or rumba. It wanted full-out ballet. It was time to tie on my pointe shoes.

CHAPTER SIXTEEN

Grand jeté

You changed wild lament into whirling dance; you ripped off my black mourning band and decked me with wildflowers. I'm about to burst with song.
—PSALM 30:11

It was June 1999, now six years into our grief. Leslie had graduated from high school and was preparing a summer regimen to keep herself in shape for the fall at Penn State. Lauren finished her junior year at Ringling and accepted an invitation for a summer internship in New Jersey with Audible, where my brother, Andy, was CEO. He and his wife, Ann, graciously invited Lauren to live with them for the summer while she worked for him.

Rob and I were approaching our 25th wedding anniversary and had planned a theatre weekend to New York City in August. In particular, I had wanted to see Bernadette Peters in *Annie Get Your Gun*. As a 12-year-old, I had been in *The Sound of Music* with her at the Mt. Gretna Playhouse, one of our community theatres. I played Brigitta; she had been brought in from New York to play Liesl. In spite of our five-year age difference, she took a liking to me and let me pal around with her, even singing and playing guitar for me one afternoon in her room at the inn on the grounds during a rehearsal break.

A young actress in my youth choir at church knew this backstory and that we were going to New York to see the show. She was ecstatic. "You need to visit with Bernadette backstage!" she exclaimed.

"She won't remember me," I insisted. "It's been 34 years! I was a kid, she's famous! I just want to see her in the show."

"You need to contact her personal assistant," she instructed. "Call the theatre. *I mean it.*"

Three days later, with what turned out to be a surprisingly easy connection with the assistant to arrange to meet Bernadette after the show, Rob and I were seated in the mezzanine of the Marquis Theatre on Broadway. The audience went wild when Bernadette stepped onto the stage. It was thrilling to see her in person again after so many years. But something deeper was happening.

When she opened her mouth to sing, and her distinctive voice harked back to those nostalgic summer theatre days, another grief that had been patiently waiting for me for 37 years was triggered and dislodged from my interior. It came rolling out in tears.

"Daddy," I had said when I was nine, "I want to be an actress." I was outside with him on the front lawn of our house, the sound of his clippers swooshing methodically at the base of an apple tree.

"Nah, that's no life for anyone," he said, yanking a tough weed with his bare hand. *Snap*. And that was that. I took him at his word, even when I was approached to try out for the Gretna production, even when I landed leads in the senior play and musical in high school. Those were fun school activities, but it was settled in my head. Acting would never be a career choice.

Seeing Bernadette startled all that awake in me again. Visiting with her afterward was great fun. She said she recognized my smile. She wondered about the Amish. She asked me if I was doing any theatre and what in the world "church music" was. She was gracious and lovely, and it was a total kick to have tourists' flash cameras on *Rob and me* as we walked out the backstage door.

But it was this grief that had been hibernating for years that had my attention, that was now a pied piper doing a full-out jig. I bought a CD of Bernadette's solo Sondheim concert at Carnegie Hall, and when we got home, I played it over and over again—especially the song, "Not a Day Goes By." It evoked not only my grief about Kelly, but also my unfulfilled longings in a raw, flesh-laid-bare kind of way that the church songs I'd been steeped in had not. Here was gut-wrenching *lament*. Why had I been so closed off from secular music all these years? Why did this music feel so much more honest than all the praise songs? I nursed every ancient yearning in my bones, and then sank down to my knees. "God, what's going on here?"

Out of the blue, I heard deep in my spirit, *Go look up NYU on the Internet.* It was odd, because I had never *ever* thought about New York University before and didn't know the first thing about it. Nor was I used to hearing strong, compelling words like that in my spirit. That simple phrase would unlock more desire and more possibility, and cause more heartache, upheaval, and joy in my marriage than nearly anything else in our lives.

While I had thought I wanted to be an actress, by this point in my life, age 46, I knew that I didn't have the kind of singing voice, dance training, or body type to succeed in that competitive world. But the first thing I found on the Internet when I looked up NYU was a month-long, masters-level, summer musical theatre writing program. It was a unique convergence of my particular skills and interests in composing, writing, and theatre—perhaps even closer to my artistic soul than acting had been. I had had a symbolic dream a few months prior to this. Now everything seemed to come together and make sense.

"What would you think," I asked Rob excitedly, "if I'd go away next July, just for the month, to study musical theatre writing at NYU?"

He thought it through financially and said, "I could actually see you doing that. I think we could probably make it work."

I went back upstairs to our computer to read more about the program. And then I clicked on another link, and up popped the thing that would nearly derail our relationship. There was also a *two-year* masters-level program. While I had thrown my dart on the outside of the circle with the July program, now I had hit the bullseye in my soul.

To go away for that long at this point in our marriage— could we endure that? How would we manage the exorbitant tuition? Even with Leslie's full ride, it made no sense for a couple finishing off paying their daughter's last year of college and working to pay off their mortgage to do something this outlandish at such an expensive school.

But I had been underwater with grief for too long. I needed *air.*

And I felt *called.*

The only way for Rob to deal with my inexplicably fierce and intense passion was to tell me to go ahead and apply for the program. He was a counselor at a high school. He knew a thing or two about college applications, and we both knew that NYU accepted only 20 people into this program. While he didn't say it at the time, he didn't honestly think I'd get in with my age and lack of theatre writing experience. Better for him if *they* said no to me, he thought.

By this time, Leslie was settled at Penn State, and I worked hard to create musical work samples to finish my application. I finally sent it off in mid-October. On Sunday morning, October 24, I had just finished playing the final song for the third church service when the church administrator slipped in through the side door, put her hand on my shoulder, and leaned close to my ear to say there was an emergency call for me at the receptionist's desk.

My sister Abby was on the line. "Ann called and said Andy was playing basketball this morning and had a heart event," she said slowly. I immediately pictured our 6'4", 40-year-old brother running around the court in a pick-up game, basketballs thumping on the wood floor and swooshing through the nets, his cheeks flushed with trademark red streaks. "He's in the hospital."

"How is he?" I asked. "What happened?"

She paused, and then said quietly, "He didn't make it." I put my arms on the counter, dropped my head on top of them, phone still up to my ear, and held on for dear life. "I haven't been able to reach Mom and Dad," she continued. "Could you go over and tell them in person?"

I felt Rob's hand on my shoulder. Some others had gathered as well, and after I hung up, I fell into them for strength. Then we gathered our things and drove to the retirement village where my parents lived.

Their car was gone, so we let ourselves into their cottage, where I called every single person I could think of who might know of their whereabouts. But no one had any idea where they were. We sat down on their sofa, my stomach in a vise, and waited for another hour and a half before we saw them pull into the driveway.

They had been out for a drive to see the fall foliage on this crisp October afternoon and were delighted to see us. "Well, this is a surprise!" my mother exclaimed as she came into the kitchen. I cannot describe the awful space between their beaming, hopeful faces and my anguished one, between their not knowing, and then their knowing. At their ages of 77 and 72, how could I possibly hand them the membership card to a club that required your very child as an initiation fee? Could they withstand the shock?

The sky was an inky clear blue, and the moon in full phase as Rob drove my parents and me to New Jersey that night. Abby and her husband, living more at a distance, drove separately. Seated in the backseat, my mother and I mostly exchanged words of disbelief, as well as excruciating concern for Ann and their three children, just 9, 5 and 3. I thought of the prayer Mom had told me about when we kids were little, how one night during a bad snowstorm Dad was hours late home from traveling for work, and how she pleaded with God to keep him safe and to keep him alive until we were fully raised adults. Now, Ann was thrust into the exact same position Mom had feared the most.

I felt at a loss to help my parents. I had grown up marveling that two such elegant, reserved, and accomplished people had given birth to someone with an emotionally expressive world as large as mine. I had wanted them to better understand my grief journey. But I didn't want them to have to understand *like this*.

I stared forlornly out the side window, my contact lenses caked with salt and my heart knifed open by the moon's sharp silver blades. I thought of Andy recording me reading my book for Audible the summer before, and how he had turned off the mic and cried with me whenever I had to stop and regain my composure. I thought of his stories about how Lauren and he would have great conversations after dinner just two months ago, drinking milk and eating brownies on the back patio. My hand rested lightly over my mother's. It wasn't the time for words anyway. We were all in too much shock.

Andy's death punched Lauren hard in the gut. It compounded grief for Leslie, who was already in the process of absorbing the loss of two fellow Penn State students who'd just been killed in an accident. The next year her former teammate Katie, the gymnast at the University of New Hampshire, would die of a pulmonary embolism.

Losses were overlapping in a wrenchingly compressed period of time, till suddenly we weren't sure what or for whom, exactly, we were grieving. It just all hurt. And those losses changed us in powerful ways. Leslie said during one phone call, "If life's going to turn out like this, why do we even bother anymore? We're just all going to die anyway."

But while loss, like a wildfire, devastates the landscape of the heart, grief is like the force inside seeds that relies on fire to break their dormancy. Without realizing it, there can be an explosion of energy and new life that defies logic.

That energy propelled Lauren to take more risks than she might have done otherwise—including backpacking across Europe with a friend after college graduation and tandem-parachuting over the Swiss Alps. I was feeling a similar kind of energy. I had been exchanging real letters with stamps with my brother for the last six years. He knew I was considering the NYU program and was rooting for me to get in. Now I wanted to go not just for me, but also for him.

Five months later, perhaps to Rob's relief, but to my crushing disappointment, I got a rejection letter from NYU. While Andy's death had knocked a certain wind out of me for life as usual, there was still that *calling*. Fueled by the worst pain, that seed was breaking in me and wanted to root. That June, I resigned my job and went to New York City to do the summer program at NYU.

Rob settled me into a dorm suite I would share for the month of July with a 19-year-old from the UK. As we said goodbye, we agreed he'd bring the girls up to visit in two weeks.

Two days later, along with another student from California, I showed up for the first day of class at the Graduate Musical Theatre Writing Program. The receptionist greeted us and said, "May I help you?"

"We're here for the summer musical theatre writing program," we told her. She looked at us in a moment of stunned confusion. Then it dawned on her, and her face went ashen.

"I'm so completely, utterly embarrassed," she said. "I remember now. The two of you had enrolled so much earlier than the others, and when we canceled the course due to low enrollment, I forgot to include you on my call list. I'm so terribly, *terribly* sorry."

I had just resigned my full-time job and uprooted my life to get there. It felt like another rejection. But I was oddly okay with it. Leslie had sent me off to NYU with the timely little book, *Who Moved My Cheese,* which I had just finished reading. So, as I walked back to my dorm, I thought of the mice in the story who, when their cheese ran out, quickly re-routed and scurried around the maze to find a new stash, rather than put all their hope in one pile of dwindling cheese.

I got back to my room, and my phone rang. It was the department head. "I'm very sorry about the mix-up," she said. "I talked with the Provost. We can offer you the chance to take any other course you want at NYU."

"Thank you," I replied, "but I really don't want any other course. I came here specifically for this." I looked out the window onto Third Avenue, and lo and behold, right across the street from my room was The East Village *Cheese* Shop.

This couldn't be a coincidence.

CHAPTER SEVENTEEN

Discernment

May you defer all decisions to the mind of love, trusting
its economy, its government, its vision of who you are.
— David Teems

"The only thing I can offer you, then," the department head continued, "is the same course as the masters level you were planning to take, only a much more intensive version with cream of the crop high school juniors and seniors."

Other people my age may have thrown in the towel right then. But I loved teenagers. I had just finished a June choir trip with 40 of them. "I'll do it," I said, without hesitation.

The next weeks were a blur of challenge and exhilaration. The intensity of this program matched my blazing hunger, and I began to be glad the other one had been canceled. If the program receptionist had notified me of the other course's cancellation like she did the others, I would have missed out on all this and probably dropped my NYU dream entirely.

I was now a 47-year-old, mixing it up and collaborating with 16- and 17-year-olds, attending Broadway and off-Broadway shows almost every night of the week, taking risks in my writing that would never have been possible in any other environment or with any other population.

One late hour on the R train, as we were immersed in lively conversation about the show we'd just seen, a male classmate, talking a mile a minute (every other word the f— word), suddenly stopped and looked at me in horror. "Oh! I'm *so sorry!* I keep forgetting you're—*a mother!*"

While I love being framed by my family, this was one time when I wasn't, which allowed me to put on my dancing shoes, kick up my heels, and live a lot more lightly and freely than I'd been doing for the last seven years.

Halfway through July, Rob and the girls came to visit. City-savvy by now, I bought them each an unlimited metro card for the day and was able to guide them all over town. Lauren, fresh out of art school, sponged up the urban scene. "I feel like if I lived here, I could do more creatively."

"You probably could," I said, secretly hoping at least one of us could live in the city I had already come to love so much.

In class later that week, our professor asked me if I'd ever considered the two-year program. Still a little bruised about the whole thing, I explained that I had applied but hadn't gotten in.

The next day he pulled me aside and said he had talked to the department head. The reason she didn't accept me was that she saw my conservative church background and didn't think I'd be happy in the program. "When all you're looking at is where people have been," he said, "it's tough to see where they want to go. She'll make a place for you in the program this fall if you want to take it."

I was grateful, relieved, and elated. But I knew six weeks would be far too little time for Rob and me to process this together, or to figure out the finances. I declined the offer and returned home as planned at the end of July. But now I had a taste of what I'd been yearning for. If not this fall, what about next?

We were now seven years post-Kelly's death. Lauren had followed up on her interest in New York City and landed a job as an illustrator at an animation company. It was exciting for Rob and me to move her into the Lower East Side so soon after I had left it. But her being there only fueled my desire to be there also. To compound Rob's distress, he now knew I was a viable candidate to get into the program the next time I applied.

Every time I brought it up, he'd look away, as if my gaze were laser surgery cutting a precise new hole in his heart again and again. We wrestled with this like nothing else. In Gordon T. Smith's book, *Listening to God in Times of Choice: The Art of Discerning God's Will*, I had read about the Quaker tradition of a "clearness committee," used for the purpose of helping a person or couple find clarity around a leading, to discover whether they should move forward with a matter, wait, or take other action. "What would you think about forming our own clearness committee?" I asked him one day.

He agreed it was an interesting idea. So, we invited three couples over for dinner to speak into our lives about this. We prepared a sheet of the issues to be considered and sent it to them ahead of time. After dinner, we sat in a circle and asked them to reflect back to us the dynamics of our relationship in regard to this issue.

A lot was said that Saturday night. But the thing that lodged in my heart like a brick was, "You guys just don't have a shared vision for this."

My heart quietly crashed, although I tried not to show it. I had told Rob I'd accept whatever they told us, and that I wouldn't beg anymore. We thanked our friends for coming, said our goodbyes, and I turned to go clean up the kitchen. I didn't want him to see the tears oozing, or to feel manipulated by them.

That night before bed, Rob said, "I'm exhausted. Can we talk about this more tomorrow?"

The next day at church, Rob took his place behind the drum set for worship. I sat in the back as we sang a song about how all things were possible with God. While I had loved this joyful song, this time I couldn't even sing it because I no longer had faith to believe it was true. After lunch I went for a long walk by myself so Rob wouldn't see the deep disappointment washing out of me in torrents.

When I got back, I flipped on a random movie called *Music of the Heart,* which turned out to be about a music teacher who moved to New York City, of all things. It made everything hurt even more.

After dinner, Rob was finally ready to talk. "I know you're disappointed."

"How can I not be?" I said, trying to keep my voice even. "The guidance we were seeking was pretty unanimous."

Then he shocked me by saying, "Well, they're not the final word on this. The jury's still out for me."

We agreed that we needed more time to process. Meanwhile, I would go ahead and apply again for the next year. Now we had more months to consider what to do. We also counseled with Pastor David, but, month after month, we repeatedly reached the same impasse. I was simply unwilling to go if Rob wasn't on the same page with me about it. It wasn't that he was forthcoming about his dissent. It was his pained silence that spoke the loudest.

That winter, like we had the winter before, we went to Penn State to see Leslie's home meets. Then early March rolled around, and this time it wasn't a thin letter that came in our mailbox from NYU. It was a thick envelope.

We were out of time to make the decision. We met with David again for one more session, but Rob still didn't feel at peace about it. I was worn down from wanting this so much. It was time to accept that it just wasn't meant to be, and to stop pushing. I called the department head to decline admission.

Three days later, on a Saturday night, we were sitting in a local theater during intermission for the play, *Inherit the Wind*. I was looking through the Playbill, commenting that I might like to take one of the theater's acting classes. By this point I had come to terms with not going to New York and was seeking something else to assuage my new yearnings. I knew, had the shoe been on the other foot, that I would have had as great, or greater, difficulty releasing Rob for two years. This was the ask of a lifetime. And with all his girls gone, he'd be alone in the house with just the dog. What was I thinking? I had put the poor guy through hell with all this. Maybe I misheard the calling.

The lights blinked off and on for the second act to start. Then, with less than a minute before the play would resume, Rob pointed to my program and quietly said, "No acting classes. That's Plan B." I looked at him in disbelief. "You need to do Plan A."

I couldn't believe what I was hearing. "Are you saying—?"

He looked toward the stage as the lights dimmed to black. "I guess I am."

By that point I had buried my dream so securely underground, I wasn't sure how to pick it up again. That night and all the next day, I checked with him again and again to be sure he was really, truly, in favor of me going—of *us* doing this. Though I had pushed hard, I wasn't going to do it if it wasn't a *we* decision. There was too much at stake.

"You'd better call them first thing tomorrow morning," he said. "They might have already given your spot to someone else."

I called the department head the next morning. The spot was still mine for the taking.

In the next weeks I scrambled to apply for grants, loans, and scholarships to make this endeavor more feasible. For extra income, I secured a job in the communications department of Eastern Mennonite Missions, where I met a pastor named Keith Blank. He knew I was working there just for the summer and that I was headed to NYU in the fall. But he knew little else about me.

My last assignment with EMM was to cover a large missions event at a local church on Sunday evening, August 26, just six days before I would move to Manhattan. I asked Rob if he wanted to come along, and he said yes. By now we were moving in sync with this plan, but one unresolved issue remained. In the past year since I had resigned my church music position, we had opted to leave the church to allow the person who replaced me time to adjust to the position. So we were essentially churchless, and along with that came the deep regret that there was no service in which we could have a community pray for us before embarking on this huge endeavor. It was the riskiest thing we'd ever done.

We took seats in a pew about two-thirds back from the front. I clicked the top of my ballpoint pen and flipped open my reporter's notebook. Pastor Keith came to the platform and opened the service. "We are gathered tonight to send off these fine young people to mission projects around the world. But tonight's service isn't just for them. It's for their parents and"—his last words caught my heart—"everyone else in attendance."

He went on to tell us that it would be the Holy Spirit in charge this night, not him, and that during the whole evening there would be a few people stationed along the sides of this large auditorium who would receive anyone, *for any reason*, who needed prayer, and that we should feel free to go to any one of them at any time during the service.

I wished we could've gone to one of those people and been prayed for. I wished I could've poured out my fears about destroying our marriage by what I was about to undertake. I wished I could've expressed my anxiety about even being able to compete in the program. But I was there on assignment, and my job was to stay put and write objectively about what was happening, not twist it for my own personal needs.

Toward the end of the service, I scribbled a note to Rob: *What would you think about asking Keith to pray for us after the service is over?*

He wrote back: *Good idea.*

My heart broke open with relief at this thought. After the last song, Keith gave the final blessing, and Rob and I walked down the aisle to the front to catch him before he left.

But in the dispersing crowd, he seemed to disappear into thin air. We turned around to scan in detail nearly a thousand people milling about and chatting with one another, trying to find him, but to no avail. The crowd gradually thinned out until it was only Rob and I standing there, like we had just missed the train to our next destination. "I guess he had another engagement," I said, crushed. "He's a busy man."

"Let's go," Rob said. We headed out the center aisle and had nearly reached the back door when Pastor Keith suddenly burst through it, nearly colliding with us.

"Keith!" I exclaimed. "We had been hoping to find you!" He is a man of intensity and purpose and seemed to have forgotten something on stage, so I blurted out my request fast and furiously: "Would you be willing to pray for us? I'm leaving for New York on Saturday, and we—"

"Say no more!" he commanded, holding up his hand to stop me. "The Holy Spirit already told me about this."

Tears sprang to my eyes as he shepherded us away from the door and laid hands on both of our heads and poured out words we will never forget: "God wants you to know first and foremost that your marriage will *thrive*. It is common in developing countries for couples to separate while one or the other leaves for further education. You are no different. God has his hand on both of you. You are not to worry.

"Lisa, don't take this the wrong way, but God is calling you to be a *mole*. You are going underground for a while to learn skills that will one day become gifts to the kingdom. Rob, you will be sustained in more ways than you can imagine as you lovingly support Lisa from home." Then he gave us a blessing, his words cascading over us with grace and encouragement. When he hugged us both at the end, we could barely speak. We had been given more than we asked for.

Six days later, Rob helped me move into a studio apartment I would sublet for the first year on the corner of Fifth Avenue and 14th Street in Manhattan. The agreement was that I would also take care of the owner's cat, a black feline named Mr. Brown. Rob and I had matching calendars and had carefully marked the holidays when I would be able to get home, and a few weekends when he would take the train to see me. And, of course, there was the entire summer between program years when we'd be together.

But after we arranged my things in the apartment, the reality of my decision set in hard. I started to cry as he prepared to leave. "I'm not sure I can do this," I whimpered, now realizing the full import of what I had so desperately been asking for these last 15 months. How could I now push out of my daily life my mainstay, my support, my love? I buried my face in his shoulder and clung to him.

"Don't even start," he said, pulling away and gripping my shoulders. "After all you put me through, you are STAYING." He was, by now, entirely supportive. At first he had feared that, had he said no to my going, I might have resented him for the rest of our marriage. But now he was fully and genuinely committed with me to doing this. He had played drums in the same summer stock theatre where I met Bernadette Peters. He knew the scores to more musicals than I, and he had a strong theatrical and production bent to his personality. He would live all of this *with* me.

One day way in the future, I would beg him to tell me how I could support his dreams, so I could give back to him what he had so sacrificially given me. "I have no dreams," he would answer. "My mission in life is to support you." And so it's been with the pattern of our marriage, with my leaning on his great support and faithful love, and his coming to appreciate the change of pace and excitement my dreams often bring him.

But I understood none of that back then, and I panicked. "What if I change so much that we grow apart?"

He smiled smugly with a twinkle in his eye. "What makes you so sure you're the only one who's going to change?"

This was the edge of the runway. It was time for liftoff. We kissed and shared a long embrace—the kind where you can barely pull apart because you don't want to let go of what's warm, safe, and familiar. But then you have to, because that was the deal.

After he'd gone, I went outside for a walk. In front of my apartment building to the left was the business industry of midtown Fifth Avenue. To the right, just a mile and a quarter away, I had a clear shot of the majestic World

Trade Center towers, like tall, comforting redwoods in my new urban landscape.

But it was Saturday, September 1, 2001. In just 10 days, they would come crashing down, an event that would be a major turning point in world history.

CHAPTER EIGHTEEN

You don't know which way the wind blows

Loss is like a wind. It either carries you to a new destination, or it traps you in an ocean of stagnation.
— VAL UCHENDU

Leslie had just begun her junior year at Penn State, majoring in Human Development and Family Studies. Lauren and I were about two miles apart, each of us with a bird's-eye view of the World Trade Center.

On Tuesday morning, September 11, Lauren was getting ready for work when she heard a boom, and her floor shook. She thought it was from construction work across the street. Seventeen minutes later she heard another boom and looked out her east window to see what was causing all the commotion. But all of the workers were at a standstill, staring to the southwest. She took the elevator to the roof of her apartment building and saw for herself the unfolding devastation.

I had been in the shower, then drying my hair when each plane struck. I was just about ready to leave for class when she called me. "Mom, are you watching the news?" I had no radio, and my TV could only play videotapes. I had no idea what was happening. "Planes crashed into both towers of the World Trade Center. They think it might be a terrorist attack."

I strapped on my backpack, waited to take the elevator nine floors to the lobby, and raced outside to look down Fifth Avenue. Cars had stopped along the curb, doors ajar as their drivers threw one leg out to hoist themselves up on the pavement while they tried to match what they were hearing on their radios with what they were seeing in front of them. Pedestrians gathered around them, trying to listen in, stunned at the smoke billowing out of the towers.

I listened for a couple minutes, but I had a class to get to, and I wanted to be in a community of people I knew. By the time I arrived at our building 20 minutes later, only a third of us had made it in. And then, on someone's handheld radio, we heard ABC's Peter Jennings say that one of the towers had collapsed. No one could believe what they were hearing. I panicked. Was Lauren's apartment building affected? I didn't know how buildings that tall collapsed. Did they tip over? Could flying debris from that height spew a mile away and bury her building under rubble?

I couldn't reach her; by then phone service was knocked out. I raced down to the computers in the basement of our program, and while email addresses didn't automatically populate with a few key strokes on email servers back in those days, I was able to respond to a friend's incoming email. I asked her to call Rob to tell him I was okay and to ask him to email me back if he heard from Lauren.

Meanwhile, one of my classmates arrived, looking like he had seen a ghost. He fell into a chair, blurting out that he had seen people holding hands as they jumped from the burning buildings. It was all surreal. None of us could take in what was happening.

Rob soon emailed that Lauren was okay, that she had watched the towers collapse from her rooftop. She saw people exiting the city on foot over bridges and asked him if he thought she should leave, too. When I learned that Leslie was 80 miles northeast of another plane that went down in Pennsylvania, I was shaken to my core.

Subways were shut down, and Lauren lived a fairly long walk away. When our department head told us to go home, and I couldn't communicate with Lauren, I went home, hoping she could eventually reach me there. I didn't want to wander the streets toward her building in such an uncertain environment.

Yellow caution tape went up across Fifth Avenue at the end of my block, separating lower Manhattan from Midtown. NYU classes were canceled for the week. Suddenly nothing we artists were doing in the world seemed to matter anymore until, at a convocation for the Tisch School of the Arts three days later, a saxophonist stood up and, with no introduction, collectively mourned for all of us with a solo rendition of "Nobody Knows the Trouble I've Seen."

The city huddled together in spirit for a couple of weeks. My neighbors chatted with each other. Bagpipers played "Amazing Grace" on street corners. For several weeks, lines to get into churches were several blocks long. Choruses sang out heartily in public commons. Flags waved and patriotism swelled like never before.

While smoke continued to rise every day like a mournful prayer from Ground Zero, eventually my classes resumed. One afternoon a week later, we studied the song, "Sarah," from the musical, *The Civil War*. It's about a soldier who writes a letter to his wife in case he is killed in the war. The song is so moving and so heart-wrenchingly beautiful that as soon as I left the building, I couldn't hold back my tears. We had just passed September 10 (Andy's birthday), September 20 (the eighth anniversary of Kelly's death), and were approaching October 24 (the second anniversary of Andy's death). Furthermore, Andy's oldest daughter's name is Sarah, so I was primed for a good soak in a grief bathtub.

But first I had to pick up a few things from the grocery store, which meant I would take a different route home. The good thing about New York City is that no one really cares if you're crying. You can emote freely just about anywhere you want, including the checkout line at the grocery store. No one looks twice at you. It's both freeing and isolating all at once.

I bought my groceries and then walked to my apartment through Union Square Park, just north of the line of demarcation between lower and upper Manhattan. I didn't realize that here was one of the key places where families of the deceased had been gathering, posting desperate notices about their loved ones. Here was where the fences were blanketed with flags, t-shirts, and photos of missing people, and the walkways were densely lined with pillar candles and flowers—*thousands of them,* overwhelming the park, and me, with heartache.

I walked slowly through them at first, and then back in my apartment a block away, the flood came. I cried for over an hour, then called Rob, asking him to please help me stop. My homesickness for him and for my family had suddenly transformed into an immense communal lament. I was feeling for the families that lost people. I was feeling my own losses.

Rob had looked into coming to offer volunteer counseling services. He figured he might be a shoo-in since he didn't need a place to stay. But it never panned out. Many people who wanted desperately to assist in some way would've simply been more in the way than helpful.

Every day of that first semester—for 100 straight days, in fact—I would look down Fifth Avenue on my way to class and see plumes of smoke rising from Ground Zero until, finally, it stopped. Sometimes I smelled it in my apartment, a strange acrid odor unlike anything else I'd ever smelled, though more often than not I was upwind from the worst of it. One day, I went to visit the site. Cranes picked slowly through the rubble like tender, compassionate fingers, careful not to disturb the sacred cremains.

During my time in New York, Rob and I saw each other every four or five weeks, when he either came for the weekend, or I went home for a holiday or for the summer. Phone calls cost money in those days, and, because we were saving every penny we could, we arranged to talk twice a week until the girls discovered this and were horrified. They practically ordered us to talk at least three times a week.

My first year there, Lauren's second, was a rough one for her. Not only was she frustrated that her salary didn't stretch very far in the city, she was also realizing it could be an unfriendly place. The entire city was shaken to begin with, and she was liking her job less and less. Then one evening after work, on a jog around her neighborhood, she saw a man's body floating just off the shoreline of the East River. She was spooked, jaded, and missing her boyfriend. She decided to take a job near him in Connecticut.

I was having a different experience. In spite of horrific events, I was doing everything I had been yearning for, while in an artistic tribe that challenged and stretched me like never before. Just as Lauren moved out of Brooklyn, where she had relocated to save some money, I moved into it for my second year at NYU. I would pick one collaborator to work with exclusively to develop a full-length musical for a final thesis. It would be performed in a black box theater setting with professional actors.

Rob and I had wonderful, romantic dates when he came up—Grimaldi's brick oven pizza near the Brooklyn Bridge, and regular hikes over it; breakfast at Clark's Restaurant like we were Brooklyn Heights regulars; and church at the world-famous Brooklyn Tabernacle, just a 10-minute walk from my apartment.

Rob had mastered the challenge of city driving when Kelly was a patient at C.H.O.P. Now he enjoyed the adventure of maneuvering in New York City's tunnels, bridges, and jammed streets. We warmed to Brooklyn in a way we hadn't to Manhattan.

I managed to get home to join him at all of Leslie's home gymnastics meets, as well as to celebrate his wish to take a frigid dip in the ocean at Ocean City, Maryland, on his 50th birthday, January 18, while I was still on winter break. In spite of all our fears, Pastor Keith was right. Our relationship grew stronger.

At the end of my second year, my full-length master's thesis musical had its professional black box reading. A month later, I graduated, and Rob helped me move home.

Perhaps because of the backdrop of tremendous grief and hard-won experience, or maybe also because I was so focused on what I was doing and had a family to support me wholeheartedly, my experience in New York far exceeded my hopes in every way. I was more grateful to Rob for his sacrifice than I could ever possibly express to him.

Just before I graduated from NYU, Heath, a fellow Penn State student athlete Leslie had been dating for a while, hitched a ride to the University of Michigan with Rob to see her compete in the Regional Championships in women's gymnastics. They got back to their room late that night after the meet and flipped on a sports station to relax before bed.

After a while, Heath mustered up his nerve. "Mr. Bair," he said, "I love your daughter. I would like to ask her to marry me." That got Rob's attention. He muted the TV. "I was wondering if I could have your blessing." We liked Heath a lot, and by this point in their relationship, Rob had expected as much. The blessing was easy to give.

Wedding planning gave Leslie and me a chance to connect more often. Once I moved home, we did it at a distance since her intense gymnastics schedule made it necessary for her to take another semester's worth of credits. That September 20, 2003, we marked the 10th anniversary of Kelly's passing. After all we'd come through, and before Leslie got married, I thought it would be helpful to assess where we were as a family. I suggested that we go for counseling when we were all together after her graduation in December—as a sort of Christmas gift to ourselves before her May wedding.

We had never done anything like this before, nor were we fully aware of what we wanted to talk about. Rob and I had gone to a family counselor named Dr. James Johnson several times before Kelly was born, so we felt confident he would be a good person to go to now.

Dr. Johnson suggested we meet on a Friday and Saturday while the girls were in town, for a few hours each day. In the car on the way to our appointment, the girls were so happy to be together again that there was a lot of laughing and storytelling. It would be a stark contrast to our trip home.

We entered his office and sat in an expectant half-circle around him. In his inimitable, gentle voice, he suggested that we pray together before we began. His prayer for our family was so tender that I was already starting to tear up. Then he said, "I'd like to open our session together with each of you telling every other family member what you love and appreciate about them."

It was a more challenging assignment than any of us anticipated. It wasn't that we doubted our love for each other. Our love was fiercely loyal and strong. But it was like an untended garden. We had taken our relationships for granted, and too much had choked in our throats along the way. Now he was asking us to express it if we could. Perhaps the greatest challenge was that not only did we have to *say* these words to one another, but we also had to *receive* them.

Dr. Johnson looked at Rob. "Will you start?"

Rob is an introvert and a self-proclaimed, task-oriented perfectionist. He doesn't like spontaneity, and he doesn't like to be put on the spot. But the prayer had warmed him, and there is no subject he's more tender about than his family.

You would have thought he had been waiting a lifetime to do this. Maybe, in fact, we all were. We just needed to be coached and given the space to do it. He poured out gentle, powerful, and loving words, first for me, then for his daughters. He melted all of us in the room, and when he finished, Dr. Johnson nodded and said, "Rob, that was incredible. This is often a tough thing for men to do."

We followed, one after another, expressing our deepest love for each other. Sometimes words came quickly in bursts with tears, sometimes more slowly with deep thought.

When we all finished—this took close to our allotted two hours—we were blessed and exhausted all at once. Dr. Johnson asked us what we might like to work on the following day. I had originally thought we would visit our mutual Kelly grief and the toll it had taken on us as a family. But what was hurting most in me was something else.

Lauren had said something to me in our session about appreciating the fact that, because of our shared time in New York City, I could understand her better, especially her recently ignited passion to take acting classes. And that was true. But during the year she and I were both living there, not even really seeing each other all that much, I had felt a growing distance from Leslie.

I couldn't put my finger on why. For much of her middle school and high school years, I'd already felt that gymnastics was mothering her more than I was. Was the distance between us now due to her intense training and travel schedule, focus on academics, and new love? Or was it because I felt guilty for being gone from the home nest and being so intensely immersed in my exhilaratingly creative world while she was still a college student? Rob's parents had done a lot to fill in while I was gone. I was appreciative, but also a little threatened by it, too.

When she got engaged, Les told me she wanted to get married in Heath's hometown at the beautiful Mercersburg Academy Chapel, two hours from Lancaster, where we lived. This only increased my perception of feeling displaced by her. I had worked at several different churches, and we were now between churches, so she saw no need to be loyal to any building—or to her hometown, since we had practically all flown from it. But I had been gone for long enough. I desperately needed a sense of home again, of gathering my chicks into the fold before they left it for good.

The summer after I graduated and she was still at Penn State, I toured church after church around town, looking to find one that would capture the aesthetic of the Mercersburg Academy Chapel. Finally, I found a smaller, more intimate version, but an incredibly lovely Episcopalian church.

"Les," I lobbied, emailing her a photo of the interior, "what do you think of this church? It's so beautiful. I just think it will be harder to plan everything from such a distance."

"Yes, it is beautiful!" she exclaimed. She came home for a weekend and we toured it together. She loved it, and we put a down payment on the date with the church. But we still had emotional work to do together.

Dr. Johnson was waiting for somebody to say something. Finally I risked it. I said I'd been feeling distance from Les in the past two years, and that my heart was hurting about it.

"Me, too," she said. I was shocked. It greatly relieved me to hear that she felt it, too. We agreed we'd start there the next day.

Counseling is exhausting. Our session of appreciation was most meaningful, but all the crying had drained us. Having a night to sleep on a foundation of expressed love and trust was quite helpful before diving in the next morning.

The next day it didn't take us long to figure out why Les and I were feeling estranged from one another. While I was perceiving being shut out of her world, she was sensing that Lauren and I had established an artistic bond that she could never break into.

Dr. Johnson was immensely helpful: "There's a problem when any family member believes that there's a coalition with another family member that they feel left out of." Les needed to hear from me that I loved her and ached to be close to her, and I needed to hear that she loved me and ached to be close to me.

We all needed to affirm that there were no coalitions in actuality—not Lauren with me, and not Les with Rob's parents—and that we all appreciated each other's unique personalities, gifts, and contributions to the family. This wouldn't be the only time we'd face coalitions in our lives together. But we now had a name for it—and a solution.

Surprisingly, Kelly didn't come up much at all in these December sessions. We didn't really need to review her death as much as we needed to assess the fallout from it—and to figure out where we were on the map again in relation to one another.

CHAPTER NINETEEN

The silent member of the family

Having a good dog is the closest some of
us are ever going to come to knowing
the direct love of a mother or God.
—ANNE LAMOTT

Tucker is the one family member who may have pieced it together better than any of us. Everyone knows that dogs possess acute sensitivity to smell. Compared to humans, their olfactory powers are so exponentially strong that while people might notice if their coffee has had a teaspoon of sugar added to it, a dog can detect a teaspoon of sugar in a million glasses of water or two Olympic-sized pools' worth. They can smell bombs and drugs, detect seizures, heart attacks, and cancer, and find lost persons. Not only do they have a 10,000 to 100,000 times keener sense of smell than humans, they also have 40 times the power of humans to analyze the data they take in.

So, what's it like for a dog in a grieving family? Unlike the rest of us who came and went on grief's holy ground, he was the one who held vigil on it day in and day out, and who received us when we fell into it at the end of our day.

He was the one who took in an encyclopedia of information about us from day one. He knew each of our scents and what our slightest gestures meant. He would spend time in each of our bedrooms every night and relish all of our fingers threading through his thick collie fur on a daily basis. He tasted our cheeks, hands, and feet and knew our nuances more intimately than we knew each others'. We knew Tucker was a gift from the start. Little did we know just how powerful a gift he would become.

We had selected him from a litter of AKC-registered shelties at an Amish farm 10 months before Kelly was diagnosed. Our first family dog had lost her hearing and passed away a month prior at the age of 15. Five-year-old Kelly pleaded with us, "Can we please get a dog this time who can *hear?*"

He was sitting quietly toward the back of the pen in the barn when we arrived, shy and slightly larger than the others. A barefoot Amish girl plucked him from the squirming litter and placed him in our arms. We took turns holding him, our hearts turning to mush. We painted one of his toenails with pink nail polish, and then pulled out a post-it note to sketch the L-shaped swath of white fur on the back of his neck so we wouldn't forget which one he was.

Two weeks later the girls and I brought him home, where we gave him a flea bath, dropped a few bits of kibble onto the linoleum, and lightly tapped our fingers on the rim of his water dish. Outside, we cooed over his adorable pudginess as he sat in the grass cocking his head from side to side at every bird and butterfly, the L-shaped swath so distinctive on his back. It was August of 1991, and we were his doting pack of humans.

At his first wellness appointment, the veterinarian remarked, "This is no sheltie; this is a small collie." We didn't care; we loved his size. Within a day or two, he began to whip up our family dynamic like a beater in cake batter. His puppy zoomies sent us into hysterics, as I ran behind him with paper towels to dab up the dribbles. He lived well into his name, Tucker, because by the time he was old enough not to sleep in a crate, he managed to spend equal time on each of our beds—tuck us in, if you will—before going to sleep by himself in the corner at the bottom of the stairs.

Dogs are usually the first to know when a storm's coming, or to sense a medical crisis. But on his first birthday 10 months later, he was too young to notice. What had shaken us to the core barely made a ripple in the pool of his puppyhood: Kelly has a brain tumor? *Let's play fetch!* Brain surgery in a children's hospital 70 miles away? *Treat, please!* Six weeks of radiation and then a year of chemo? *Local firehouse siren! Owwwwwooooooh!*

Lauren grabbed fistfuls of mini-marshmallows to lure Tucker to her room at night. Leslie was mortified every time he chewed the crotch out of a new leotard. When Kelly and I were in the hospital, Rob and the girls called us on the phone so we could hear him howl in the background, and brushed off enough of his fur to stuff into a baggie for their next visit, so Kelly could nuzzle it against her cheek.

During respites at home from the hospital in the winter, we would all cringe when we saw Tucker chomping on his frozen turds in the back yard. Thus, he grounded our heads and hearts when they spun out of control with fear and anxiety.

When we brought Kelly home from the hospital on the last day of her life, Tucker settled down next to the sofa where she lay in our family room and stayed there until she passed a few hours later.

Weeks after her death, I was home alone one evening and sat down to play the piano in our living room, with only the soft light of Christmas candles in the windows. I had often accompanied Kelly as she would sing "At the End of the Day" from *Les Miserables* in a defiant, boisterous, little voice worthy of the Broadway cast of adults, and then "Castle on a Cloud" as winsomely as any six-year-old child could. But on that night, I whimpered through the heartbreaking "On My Own," because that's how I felt. The words garbled as I sang through my tears, but I couldn't stop.

And that's when I realized I wasn't alone. I looked down, and there was two-year-old Tucker, his head pressed firmly on my thigh. I took my fingers off the piano keys and embraced him, crying into his neck. He was slightly claustrophobic and not much for hugs, but he didn't squirm out of my grasp. That was the night he earned his soul. And while his function during her illness was Court Jester, now he was Minister of Grief.

I can't begin to know all he meant to Rob, Lauren, and Leslie during the worst of those early years, but I don't doubt his fur absorbed an ocean of bewilderment, grief, and emotional chaos.

Tucker knew every private room in this era of our lives. He was like a kid who knows the lay of his best friend's house because he goes in and out of it to play every day, into rooms that adults would never casually show each other.

Dogs are also known to experience separation anxiety in their first years, and to experience variations of that anxiety as they mature. What did he feel as, one by one, his packmates began to leave—first Kelly, then Lauren and Leslie to college?

A week before I left for NYU, when he had grown into a true soulmate at 10 years old, I lay on the floor beside him and tried to explain what was going to happen. I would miss Rob and Tucker terribly, but Rob had made the decision with me. How could I make Tucker understand?

"I'll always be with you in spirit, my sweet boy, and back to visit on holidays," I said, stroking his ears and looking him deep in the eye, channeling my best dog-whispering self. "Don't forget me, okay? Please take really, really good care of Rob for me, will you?" I gave him final kisses on my favorite three spots on his head, the soft indentations above each eye, and then tracing with the tip of my nose the white line of fur between his eyes before planting a final kiss on his forehead. Then I picked up his front paw. Rob had pointed out to me one time how sweet the bottoms of his feet smelled. I took in a good whiff. "I like the way you smell, too, boy."

I've always been fascinated by Tucker's sense of spatial awareness as to where everyone was in the house at any given point. Shelties are from the herding breed, of course, and those dogs are known to keep track of anything from sheep to walnuts. But because he never seemed to favor any one of us, he seemed more gentlemanly about his oversight of all of us. When everyone was home and in their bedrooms on the second floor, he would sleep at the bottom of the stairs. When it was down to just Rob, he slept on the floor beside Rob every night of my absence. When I returned home for good, and it was just the two of us, he slept on the floor at the end of our bed. He was an innate and gifted mediator of affection.

At Christmastime two years later, around the time of our family therapy session, Tucker was 12½ and beginning to lose his hearing, so we began to clap to get his attention. About the same time, Les got her diploma, and wedding planning was in full swing.

On Monday, March 4, 2004, just two months before the wedding, I was preparing lunch when I heard Tucker struggling to get up off the kitchen floor. "What's the matter, boy?" I soothed. "Do you want to go outside?" I patted my legs to coax him toward the door.

Tucker tried again, then fell helplessly back down. I tried to lift him to carry him outside myself, but he weighed over 55 pounds, and I couldn't do it.

I called Rob to come home, and we spent the day at two veterinary clinics. At the second one, a specialty clinic, he was diagnosed with severe pancreatitis. The veterinarian looked at us and paused. We knew it wasn't good news. "Worst case I've ever seen, I'm afraid. I'm very, very sorry."

Rob gently scooped him up in his arms and laid him in the back of our Jeep, his body leashed to an IV. He lay still as stone. As we drove back to our local veterinary clinic, we both knew we wouldn't be able to financially afford lengthening his time with transfusions for uncertain results, at best.

It was a Monday afternoon, exactly as it had been for Kelly as we brought her home from the hospital in the back of our car. The synchronicity pierced us, and the grief was suffocating. We were drowning in sorrow, and Tucker was suffering.

I regret that we didn't call the girls to draw them into our decision, at least to let them know Tucker's condition and give them time to absorb his illness before we delivered news of his death. But it had all happened so fast, and since we didn't have cellphones at that point, it would've taken a while to track them both down.

We planted last kisses on his forehead and stroked the length of this incredible and so deeply-loved animal, who had absorbed our family's pain with so much unconditional love and mercy. "Thank you," we whispered in his ear. "We'll love you forever." And then, falling on him in tears, we choked into his ear, *"Go get Kelly."*

CHAPTER TWENTY

Grief and praise

Praise is Grief's eternal freight train, forever
hauling the vision of life's bigger picture
from stars whose light hasn't got here yet.
——MARTÍN PRECHTEL

After her December graduation, Leslie took a short-term job at Penn State during the winter and spring months. When she finally moved home a couple of weeks before the wedding, she would tell me that coming into the house was like hitting a wall of quiet. No "howly hello" from Tucker, no clicking of his nails on the kitchen floor or banging against the wood blinds at the back door to go out.

She set her things down on the kitchen table that first day back and looked askance at his tan-colored water bowl on the floor in its normal place in the corner against the pantry. "Mom," she said, pointing to it. "What's *this*?" Tucker had been gone for over two months. His bowl was half full of water.

I confessed to her that I would refill it every time the water evaporated, that it helped my heart somehow. As only an adult daughter can do, especially a bride-to-be imagining people from her wedding party coming through the house in a few weeks, she put her arm around me and said, "I get it, Mom, I really do." She picked the bowl up off the floor and gently walked me over to the sink to empty it out. "But maybe it's time to move on, don't you think?"

Her energetic and assertive arrival helped shepherd my heart into a new era, which officially began two weeks later on the warm and sunny morning of her wedding, May 22, 2004. Joyous major family events accentuate loss—especially in photographs. We had envisioned Tucker in the pre-wedding photos, and of course Kelly would've been a bridesmaid. Les wanted to tag single pink carnations with *Remembering Kelly* to hand out to guests arriving at the church. It felt good to work on them together, and to celebrate her memory.

Lauren had flown in from Portland, Oregon, where she now lived and worked as an illustrator at an animation company. During Kelly's illness, she and Leslie had formed a tight bond against the forces happening in our family, and now, cross-country from one another, they never had enough time together. They both cried over their speeches at the rehearsal dinner, then spent too much of the night laughing and catching up.

After they got their hair done the next morning, Leslie confided in me that she didn't feel well. I figured it was from excitement and lack of sleep. "What have you eaten today?"

"A grape and a chip," she admitted. I tried to get her to drink and eat more, but she couldn't, and before we knew it, it was 2:30 p.m., a half hour before the ceremony. "I feel better now," she said, taking a deep breath. She looked at my furrowed brow. "Really, Mom, I do."

At 3:00 p.m., Heath's mother and I lit the family unity candle at the front of the church, and the processional began. Heath came out with his groomsmen, handsome and ready, and while I memorized every detail of the ivory wedding gown and cathedral-length veil Leslie had picked for this special day, no one can prepare a mother for the moment when she sees it on her lovely daughter coming down the aisle.

Pastor David smiled broadly as he stood in front of the anxious young couple. "Take a deep breath," he said to them with a huge smile, and everyone laughed and relaxed. Within 15 minutes, the knot was legally tied and we acquired a son-in-law.

Lauren regaled the guests at the reception with her maid of honor toast, telling a funny story about when Heath mistook her for Leslie at the bowling alley. She also put together such a professional video of Leslie and Heath's story that the DJ whispered to me, "Has she ever thought about doing this for a living?"

And then he switched on the music, and the Penn State women's gymnastics team took to the floor. We quickly followed, dancing our hearts out in a release we deeply needed. This was branches in full bloom for our family, and a time to dance.

Overnight, it seemed, our house was swept clean of everything but Rob and me and the furniture, and a dining room table stacked with wedding gifts we would eventually transport to Leslie and Heath in Chicago.

One evening that summer, moonlight beckoning from the window, I went outside for a walk. At the end of the driveway, I heard a barely audible squeal coming from behind the garbage bins in our neighbor's yard across the street. A new family had just moved in, and we knew they had a black border collie named Skye. It was pitch-dark except for the lamppost light and the glow of a half moon. I moved closer to the sound. Then I saw her as my eyes adjusted to the darkness, her black body trembling and squirming close to the ground in a submissive posture. I knelt down and stroked her. "Well, hello. So very nice to meet you, Skye."

Skye soon became the neighborhood mascot. Obsessed with fetching tennis balls, she insisted, from inside her invisible electric fence, that *everyone* walking by owed her a few tosses. Most people complied because no one could resist her sweet affection and enthusiasm.

But that first night in the darkness, she ignored her tennis balls lying in the grass. She stayed present with me, nosing my face and hands as if, in one fell swoop, she was drinking in my entire life and finding immediately where it hurt. When I returned a half hour later, she was still there waiting like she had known I'd be back. As I nestled my head against her cheek, I had the distinct sense that she was picking up where Tucker left off.

Over the next seven years we would throw a gazillion balls for her. We even allowed her to sleep with us in our bed most nights when we took care of her while our neighbors were on vacation. She was well-trained and supremely intelligent. I joked with our girls that Skye would even mop our floors if we asked her to.

Les and Heath made a home in Chicago for a year, then moved back to Baltimore, where they acquired a strikingly adorable but obstinate rescue pup they tried desperately to discipline. One afternoon Les called, on the verge of tears. "Olive is such a handful," she choked. "She's definitely not Skye the Perfect Dog."

I laughed, but I knew why she was frustrated. Olive had a personality we weren't used to either. She seemed to get defiant, rather than contrite, when disciplined. "Really, Les, if it's too much, you know you can send her back." Those were the wrong words. She burst into tears.

Olive managed to keep her place in their family, and one weekend Leslie brought her up for us to care for while she visited with friends. Olive was almost full grown by now, and we were beginning to rather like her bullheaded but affectionate personality. She didn't have the extraordinary sensitivity of either Tucker or Skye, and, well, it was oddly refreshing.

That night Olive lay quietly between us while we were watching a baseball game. "She's used to sports TV, I'll bet," I said to Rob. "It seems to calm her down." Then I noticed she was trembling.

Les returned later and grew concerned, determining that we should take her to the 24-hour pet clinic. While there, she became clingy, jumping into our laps for comfort, which was a whole different side of her we'd never seen—and rather enjoyed.

A half hour later, the veterinarian emerged from the examining room with a twinkle in his eye. "Olive had one boatload of poop stuck in there. I gave her an enema, and she is now much better. She'll be fine."

The dogs in our lives were a wonderful solace. But empty-nesting was particularly hard for Rob. After NYU, I had taken a few short-term jobs to help pay back my loans and catch up with new debts related to my musical's development. Then the year after Les and Heath's wedding, I took a music job at a church in Lancaster city, which satisfied my longing to be back in New York. The smells, the sirens, the restaurants, and coffee shops were pretty nice here, too, I thought. I began to feel that urban tug—and to look at our local city real estate listings. It was just for fun, at first. But then I asked Rob, "Would you even consider moving into the city?"

"Maybe after I retire, and not unless we can find a double garage," he said. We had lived in the city when we were first married, but our home of the last 24 years had been in the suburbs, right next to the cemetery where Kelly was buried. It seemed almost blasphemous to leave it. Up to this point there was no way I could've moved out of that house permanently or away from that cemetery. But we were visiting her grave less often now, and I was feeling less and less emotionally tethered to it. My time in New York City had also awakened my urban side. My living preferences were changing.

During that time my father's health began to decline, and for the last three years of his life, he lived apart from my mother in an entirely different skilled care facility. One day he passed out in the bathroom and was put to bed. He never got out of it again. Ten days later, he passed away. It was a tender and poignant loss, as would be the deaths of our remaining three parents in the 11 years to come. But saying goodbye to them was also more in the natural order of things than our family funerals had been thus far.

In the fall of 2009, a colleague approached me about giving my musical a fully-staged and orchestrated world premiere with our local opera company, of which he served as president. He was also a developer downtown and got me to thinking more seriously about real estate.

About a year after the production, Rob retired, and we decided to buy the last unbuilt lot in an association of city townhouses—the one my colleague and his wife had considered building on for their retirement. Several months later Leslie announced that she was pregnant. She and Heath were house-hunting, too, and Lauren had already moved to L.A. the previous year to further a promising acting career.

We were moving with less resistance now to the ebbs and flows of the waves of our lives. Like hermit crabs on the beach, we had all reached a point where we had outgrown the old shells on our backs. As geographically far apart as we all were now, it was a separation with joy, so different from the emotional separation in early grief. Now, new life was on the horizon as we eagerly awaited our first grandchild.

CHAPTER TWENTY-ONE

More people on our team

Something very beautiful happens to people when their world has fallen apart: a humility, a nobility, a higher intelligence emerges at just the point when our knees hit the floor.

— MARIANNE WILLIAMSON

Since I would be receiving my mother's grand piano when we moved, Les asked if she could have our studio upright piano and living room furniture. One evening in early September of 2011, I got the strongest feeling. "Rob," I said. "We have to get this furniture to Les and Heath *tomorrow.*"

They were moved into their new house, but they had nothing substantial to sit on. I couldn't imagine what she'd sit on to nurse a newborn without a sofa in front of the TV. She wasn't due for another week, but we had a U-Haul and were basically ready to go.

The next afternoon, while Rob, Heath, and a few of his friends brought the things into the house, Les and I chatted on her back patio. "I just can't imagine I'll ever have a mother voice," she lamented.

"Oh, don't worry about that," I said. "Trust me, you'll be surprised how quickly that will come!"

She stroked her swollen mid-section. "How do you know when your time comes?" There was a look of slight discomfort in her face. It seemed to me like things might be brewing.

That next morning, September 4, 2011, at 3:20 a.m., we got the call and jumped into our clothes to travel to Towson, Maryland. Amid normal concerns that the birth would go smoothly for Les and baby, we chatted excitedly about what we wanted our grandparent names to be. "Grammy and Grampy" were already taken on Heath's side, so we opted for something altogether different—"Lolli and Pop." (We had a feeling we'd be suckers for our grands.)

Heath and Les wanted to be gender-surprised, so when Hudson was born, it was a natural joy for all of us. But after raising three girls, Rob and I found it to be a unique treat to hold a baby boy in our arms. We spent the morning with them, and then Les and I conferred about when I'd come to help with the baby at their home. We kissed their new little family goodbye and returned home to pack and get some sleep.

The next morning I awoke from a short and terrible dream: *I am carefully bathing my new grandson in the bathroom sink. His skin is glistening in the warm bubbly water, and he is happy. Suddenly he slips out of my grasp and I cry in horror as he sinks below the surface of the water. I cannot retrieve him.*

I awoke short of breath, inconsolably upset. Intellectually, I could attribute this dream to my fear of losing another child, of projecting Kelly's loss onto Hudson. But I felt like I did after I'd once been in a bad head-on collision. I wasn't secure on the road anymore.

Later that day I talked to a few professional friends, who concurred that the dream was my subconscious fear of losing another child. Their immediate attention and professional insight relieved the huge emotional burden, so that by the time I arrived a day later to help with the baby, I could set aside the fear and jump right into enjoying supporting Heath and Leslie and my new grandson.

When Hudson was three years old, and our new granddaughter Hadley had recently turned one, I was watching Hudson sit up high at the kitchen counter and munch away on a snack I had just made for him. "I love you, Hudson," I said, with all the tenderness of a smitten grandmother. And then it just came out: "Do you love me?"

He looked at me thoughtfully, cocked his head a little to think even harder, and then crushed my heart. "No," he said.

"Well, who *do* you love?" I asked, trying to stay positive.

"MommyDaddyHadley," he said, as if they were one person.

I named his other grandparents and family members, including Pop (who by now had become Poppa), and he nodded that he loved all of them. But not me.

Les was horrified when she came home and I jokingly told her that her son had broken my heart. "What?" she exclaimed, then immediately called him from another room. "Hudson, come here! You love Lolli, right?"

Just as I was protesting her doing this, he shook his head no and ran into the next room. I laughed it off, telling her not to worry, that it was a ridiculous question to ask a three-year-old. But like a grain of sand in an oyster, it worked in me. "Don't try so hard," Rob said. "Let his feelings come to you."

Rob was relaxed and cool with Hudson. Admittedly, I was overprotective, more like a guard dog. I determined early on that *nothing* would happen to this child on my watch. Lauren had been in a highway collision with Rob's parents when she was 17. It wasn't their fault, but her head had come within six inches of the front wheel of the other car. I hadn't quite recovered from it. I didn't want to put Heath or Leslie through that—ever.

A professional friend, who knew of my nightmare when Hudson was born, offered more solace. "These things come to the surface to find healing," she said. "Hudson may be picking up on the energy of your overprotectiveness." He was a sensitive kid, for sure; I loved that about him. But maybe she was right.

From that day on, I intentionally relaxed and pulled back from him. I didn't assault him with hugs when we arrived or demand a hug from him when we left. And sure enough, our relationship changed. We hung out more easily, and he made it clear, by his smiles and laughter, that we were in an easy and natural place together, just as we should be.

Two years later, we welcomed Holden into the family. By this point Lauren had become "Aunt Bubbles," and our reunions, whenever possible with all of us all being at such a distance, continued to be the joy of our existence.

At our large extended family gatherings, we had often felt diminished by having lost a member of our family. In Rob's words, we didn't have "enough people on our team." Now, we were filling out a little, recovering from that visceral sense of amputation.

We decided to try a fall family beach vacation in October of 2016. It didn't start off with ideal weather, because a low-pressure system, driven by the northernmost bands of a hurricane, had started to bear down on the mid-Atlantic. We had driven three hours and unpacked our gear in wet and gusty winds. After finally getting settled and eating a spaghetti supper all together, five-year-old Hudson was raring to go. "Lolli, can you please take me to see the ocean?" he pleaded.

We were just two houses away from the beach, and since there was a brief lull in the rain, I easily said yes. "It's chilly and windy," I said, pulling his blue hoodie over his head and tightening the strings on mine, figuring we had at least 15 minutes before the sky unloaded again. He flew out the door and ran ahead, skittering over the boardwalk and leaping onto the dunes between the sand fences. I followed as quickly as I could, shouting into the bracing wind, "Hud, wait for me! The waves are really rough—don't get too close to the water!"

It was just an hour before dark, and the sea was agitated and foaming at the mouth. Gray clouds churned ominously overhead. The wind was dramatic and invigorating, and Hud took off, chasing and retreating from the sudsy white edges of the water like a human sandpiper.

We had the beach all to ourselves, and his joy was irrepressible and contagious. We laughed and kicked up sand and water, and I threw back my hood and let the wind splay my thick, layered hair into stiff, outward spikes. "Does my hair look funny?" I shouted.

His laughter penetrated through the roar of the waves. "Yes!" he shouted back. When I caught up with him later and bent down to roll up his soggy pant legs, I realized the shifting sands and divergent waves had disoriented us and pushed us pretty far down the beach. "Hud," I said, taking him by the shoulder and pointing way up the beach. "See that brown house with the yellow one beside it? Right between them is how we get back to our place. Let's keep an eye on that spot, okay?" He nodded and took off again as I nudged him northward.

I stopped to catch my breath, my arthritic back and knees reminding me it had been a *long* time since I was five years old. I studied his lithe, fleeting form, effortlessly whizzing past me like I was a stalled car on the highway. The clouds unburdened themselves a little, and our hoodies darkened with raindrops. But neither of us was ready to leave.

As the light grew even darker and the rain a little heavier, I marveled at this gift of a grandson, and then I sank so deeply into the thought that I started to cry. I felt the jaws of time clamping down on me, even as they yawned wide open for him, the weight of my life experience sinking far below the featherlight happiness of his fresh, expanding world. Would he visit me in a nursing home someday? Would he giggle to his siblings about my dementia, look on in horror at my missing teeth . . . *cry at my funeral?* Would he remember this night? Would I?

Stay in this moment! I ordered my heart. But how could I convey my deep and effusive love for him—this boy who, age-appropriately, squirmed out of my hugs and preferred high-fives?

I breathed in the energy of sand, wind, rain, and sea, and this small, darting human still looping and spinning around me. I knew I could crush him with the weight of my feelings if I wasn't careful. So, standing there at the edge of the continent, I mentally switched tracks and remembered that it wasn't just time that was moving at a dizzying pace. In just 24 hours, we would each have rotated with the earth a distance equivalent to nearly 25,000 miles, at a speed of something like 1000 m.p.h.—which meant that, in just our short time together on the beach, we would have traveled about 500 miles in space.

I felt like my heart had already gone twice that far. I willed it to come back and give him this blessing instead of a lachrymose longing:

Go, Hudson, go! Let my love lift and not ever restrain you! May all the energy in your legs, heart, and mind carry you far and bring you and the world as much joy as they're bringing you and me right now. And may you reciprocate my love not by piling it back onto me (well, maybe a little), but by passing it on to your own children and grandchildren. And like it or not, girl cooties notwithstanding, I am kissing you now, and I'll be kissing you forever, with all my love and gratitude for you.

"C'mon, buddy!" I finally shouted. "It's getting dark; time to go back." He sped past me and raced up the sloping dunes, his body not having stopped once in the half hour we were out there.

Without even looking back to confirm with me, he correctly threaded himself between the brown and yellow houses and disappeared from view.

CHAPTER TWENTY-TWO

Finding meaning

She was no longer wrestling with the grief, but could sit down with it as a lasting companion and make it a sharer in her thoughts.
——GEORGE ELIOT

It was Monday, February 11, 2008, when Rob came home after a long day at school, hung his keys on the wall, and said, "You are not going to believe this. Sit down. I have to tell you what happened today."

I turned off the burner on the stove and brought our plates to the table. "Is everything okay?"

"Yes, it's all good. Incredible, really." He took off his jacket, washed his hands, and joined me at the table. He told me about a 16-year-old student who had come into his office that morning. Having a caseload of several hundred students, this was nothing unusual for him. Conversations were always confidential and never shared with me. But this was different.

"Her name is Heather, and she was desperate to talk to me. Well, actually, she's not one of my counselees. She's also desperate to talk to *you*." She had come in fighting back tears, and then she took a deep breath and poured out her story.

Heather had skipped out of school and earned herself a four-hour detention, which she had just completed the Saturday before. Until then, she had not only been struggling academically in school, but was also depressed and riddled with fear about death and dying. Her mother suggested she spend the time in detention reading a book she'd heard about called, *A Table for Two*.

Heather explained to him that she couldn't put the book down during all four hours of her detention. "And then I couldn't stop reading it when I got home. I read it all through Sunday and into Monday morning. Mr. Bair, I have faith in God for the first time. I'm no longer afraid of dying. Then I found out that the father of the little girl in the book was right here in my high school! I knew I had to find you."

It was nearly the tenth anniversary of the book's publication, and while a myriad of people had written to tell me how it had affected them, this was the first that anyone told me about coming to faith—the fulfillment of Kelly's journal stating she felt like a missionary with a message to tell people about God's love.

At the end of her visit with Rob, Heather reluctantly asked him if he would mind telling her where Kelly was buried. After school, she and her boyfriend went to a flower shop, where she purchased a colorful bouquet and a white teddy bear to go with it.

She and her boyfriend then drove to the cemetery to search for Kelly's grave, but to no avail. Freezing from the cold, they went back to their car to get warm. Then she said, "I have to try one more time." This time she found Kelly's stone. Trembling from the cold, she laid the flowers and the bear at the base of the headstone and wrote on a tiny card, *Thank you. Love, Heather.*

A few days later, I invited Heather and her mom Lori to come to our home. Both strikingly beautiful, tanned, and looking like they had stepped out of a salon, they thanked me profusely for writing the book and gushed gratitude for my taking time to meet with them. "Please, please," I said over and over. "The honor is *mine*. You don't know how much this means to me, too."

Heather asked me about Kelly, about God, about our family. Her mother explained that their family had stopped attending church a long time ago, when Heather was a toddler. A painful circumstance had caused them to leave, and she was sorry she dropped the ball over the years and couldn't guide Heather better in her faith. We talked for two hours, marveling over every amazing detail of the divine synchronicity of our connection.

We had discovered we lived only a mile apart. As they were leaving, I said, "Heather, if you're interested in learning more about the Bible, I would be happy to teach you—if that's ever something you'd be interested in. Just think about it."

She had been secretly praying for exactly this. "I don't have to think about it—yes!" she said. Lori said she would be interested, too, so we arranged to get together on a Monday evening at their house.

For the next two years we met at their place or mine every Monday night. The two of them were spiritual sponges. Lori took meticulous notes. They opened their hearts, shared their personal challenges, and honored me like I was their pastor. Heather continued to struggle in school, but now she had coping tools—prayer, the sense of a strong advocate in God, and something sorely missing from her life—hope.

Without any encouragement on my part, Heather began visiting Kelly's grave, particularly when she was feeling low. In my daughter, she found a friend, a heavenly connection, someone to confide in. Sometimes I found notes on Kelly's grave, or small objects, and I knew Heather had been there.

One night, Lori began to cry. "I just feel so badly that you had to lose your daughter so that mine could be found." But for me, and for Kelly, I believe, it was a kind of fulfillment. I felt nothing but joy and love for these two, and a profound sense of energetic movement and healing in my own grief.

During our times together, we prayed, made fun crafts, and ate snacks. Heather eventually asked if her boyfriend and another friend could join us. We all had marvelous times together and became fast and close friends. Rob and I had suggested to Lori and Heather that they might like to attend a particular church in our area especially geared to new believers, and they immediately took to it, along with Heather's father, Bob.

At some point during those first weeks, I retrieved the bear, remarkably unscathed from the elements, and the card from Kelly's grave. "I want you to keep these," I told Heather, "as a symbol of your newfound faith."

On a bright spring morning at the end of March the following year, I went into the immersion pool at her church with Heather and her pastor the Sunday she was baptized. At the end of the service, they replayed on film in reverse slow motion the baptisms that had occurred that morning. All the beautiful water of healing and renewal flowing back into Heather's face was a stunning image I will never forget.

After two years' time, just before Heather turned 18, I had a permanent schedule conflict and had to pull out of our regular meetings. But we stayed in touch as often as we could, particularly as Heather went through some personally challenging times.

One late winter day six years later, Lori told me that Heather was pregnant. She was due on October 9. But because her baby wasn't positioned properly and didn't turn, she was scheduled for a C-section on October 5. One last ultrasound, however, revealed low amniotic fluid, so the doctor made the decision to preemptively avoid complications and deliver the baby right then and there.

Heather gave birth on September 20, 2016, at 4:35 p.m. to a beautiful baby girl she named Giuliana Lorelle. It so happened to be the day of Lori and Bob's wedding anniversary. But that's not all. It was also the exact day, and hour, of Kelly's passing. It was an exclamation point on what we all feel is our divine interconnectedness.

With no coaxing from her mother, baby Giuliana gravitated toward the bear Heather put on Kelly's grave and adopted it as her "stuffie." Now four years old, she still sleeps with it every night.

CHAPTER TWENTY-THREE

My daughters reflect

*I have found being a mother has made me
emotionally raw in many situations.
Your heart is beating outside your
body when you have a baby.*
— KATE BECKINSALE

In the beginning, Rob and I had tried to gather our family together to comfort and rebuild. But each one of us was on our own journey, trying to figure out how to keep going. Rob and I had lost a daughter. Our girls had lost a sister *and* the focus of their mom and dad, who were consumed during a large part of their critical development with their sister's illness, and now with her death.

Our emotionally distracted parenting during their critical teenage years has remained my greatest regret. It took 22 years before Lauren finally revealed that she couldn't understand why we let Kelly make the decision whether she wanted to have more chemo or not. Why hadn't we intervened to give her more months to live?

Lauren had neither seen the MRI with the four new brain tumors on all sides of Kelly's head, nor been part of the conversation with the oncology team at C.H.O.P. She didn't grasp the imminence of death or how more treatment would have compromised Kelly's ability to enjoy her last days. And she wasn't part of the discussion when we talked to Kelly about her wishes. But had we known that she was harboring those feelings, perhaps we would have been able to help her, even encouraging Kelly to wait to make the decision with the whole family until after her sisters got home.

When I began this book, planning to have our daughters read it to make comments for me to include in its final draft, I realized there was much we still hadn't talked about. Our cross-country communication is peppered now with fast-paced texts with emojis, Snapchat, Instagram, and plenty of humor. I dreaded in some ways making them plumb the depths of their own experience.

Especially hard for me was that Leslie's kids are now around the age Kelly was when she was diagnosed. Her identification with me as a mother is deep. "I don't know how you did that, Mom," she says sometimes about our experience, and I know she has put herself many times in my shoes with her own children. Why unearth all this again? Maybe, I trusted, because we now have enough distance to do so without unraveling at the seams.

When I had roughed out about a hundred pages of this manuscript, I realized my recollection of my family's experience was woefully inadequate, so I changed directions from a personal narrative and decided that this book would be more powerful as a family's, not just a mother's, perspective. I left it open-ended and printed three spiral-bound copies of what I had written so far, gave one to Rob, and mailed the others to Lauren and Leslie.

I asked them to respond to what I had written, and then to mark their copies with whatever came to mind. I looked forward to finally filling in the missing puzzle pieces of my heart, as if a quarter-century was sufficient emotional and maturational distance to talk about this. I imagined it as sitting in the audience of a play you once starred in, now with a new cast, as if experiencing the play for the first time. The idea invigorated me so much that I joked with a friend, "If this never gets published, at least it will provide some good family therapy!"

I did not expect that I would be so entirely sobered by my daughters' responses that I would retreat into myself for an entire summer, and be unable to continue with the book. I wept every time I thought of them and what they—truly lovingly, please understand—fed back to me.

Rob gave more editorial comments than anything else. "I don't need those now," I said. "I want your *emotions* about what you've read." But it was like pulling teeth.

"Honestly," he finally said, "I really don't want to delve into all of this again. I don't have the need like you do to reach out and help other people. But you should do what you feel called to do. I don't want to get in the way of that. It's really *your* story you're telling."

Lauren gave me her comments over the phone. It struck her profoundly that she was now the age Rob was when Kelly died. "I can barely take care of myself at this age; I don't know how you did this." She marveled at the passage of time, at how different our experiences were from one another, how none of us knew, back then, how our actions were impacting each other. "We were all having these private moments that no one else knew about."

Her voice rose passionately as she said, "Why *did* we all resume our activities so quickly? Why *were* we constantly catering to other people? What did we owe anyone?" There was some anger in her voice, as if this pattern, to this day, was still pinning us all to the wall.

Her natural humor flowed in and out of the conversation. A writer herself, she made a few editorial comments that made us both laugh. "You say you see God everywhere—like in your 'tiny neighbor's toothless grin.' Mom, are you living next to a *gnome?*"

She reflected more on her first weeks as a high school sophomore right after Kelly's death. She reiterated how much she feared dying at that point. "I couldn't google brain tumors back then to find out if two people in a family could both get them. But I worried all the time."

She told me that she was also sensitive to terms her peers casually threw around that would "slam into my heart in a bad way"—like "You have cancer!" or "I have a slurpy tumor" when they drank a slushy or ate ice cream too fast. She didn't remember what had caused her to cut up her blouse, but she was impassioned in telling me, "You need something from people when you're going through this that you don't know how to ask for, and they don't know how to give, and they can't get it right, and it just can't be answered. It's very lonely."

She mentioned that she was fascinated by our relationship with our grandchildren. I asked her whether she felt threatened by our proximity and relationship to them. She referred to something I'd said in a blog one time about Hudson. "You wrote that your heart 'opened back up' with his birth, 18 years after it 'sealed shut' upon Kelly's death." She paused, then added, "Mom, *I was right there all that time.*"

I tried to explain what I meant, that it was a poor choice of words, that I hadn't meant that I had closed off to her and Les. But it was useless to try. She was giving me clear confirmation for the first time about what I had feared and regretted most—that she did suffer from my unintentional neglect.

The curtain of my memory pulled back to an evening when she was seven and Leslie was four, and I was tucking them in at bedtime. Their twin beds were perpendicular to each other against the walls under the windows, each with matching, powder-blue bedspreads with a white floral etching of some sort. Kelly was an infant, asleep in the next room, and I had just kissed them both goodnight when I heard Lauren mutter something I couldn't make out.

"What did you say?" I leaned over her and peeled back the covers she had pulled over her face.

I could see her chin quiver in the semi-darkness, and I was stunned to hear these words: "I have a broken heart, and I need more love." I'm sure I scooped her up into my arms and reassured her that she was deeply loved. But I'm also sure, as a tired parent of an infant, that I didn't spend a lot of time trying to find out where her comment came from.

Now, over the phone, at a distance of 2,650 miles, I heard that seven-year-old child say the same thing about her 15-year-old self, her 20-year-old self, and her 40-year-old self, and my heart broke into a million pieces.

"Don't take this the wrong way," she laughed, "but I told Les I'm going to write a book called, *All the People My Mother Loved More Than Me.*" She named two of my significant friends at the time as titles for chapters one and two, and then I stopped her. I could see where this was going. Deeply sensitive like her, I would, of course, take it the wrong way. I didn't let on that I did, and we moved on to other phases of those grief years. But it's what stuck with me.

"She's right," Rob confirmed. "You give so much to the world, to everybody who's hurting. Sometimes you neglect the people right in front of you."

Since Lauren had made it clear that she and her sister had already talked about these things, I spoke with Les at one of Hudson's baseball games one afternoon a week later. I asked her if she felt the same way. She rushed to assure me that the root of all this was love, but that yes, she had felt it, too. She said she remembered, as a seventh-grader, coming out of her bedroom and going down the hall and seeing the back of me as I was writing my first book on our new computer in Kelly's room. "The image I remember most during that time, Mom, was of your back turned away from us."

Her words crushed me. I had asked for this. I had *wanted* to know. But now I was seeing something I hadn't seen before—that my own daughters hadn't done as well as I had thought they were doing at the time. They needed to have been more the focus of my mercy and intention, more than anyone else. Those schedules, all that running around to please the clock, the calendar, other people. Why didn't we *stop*?

Neither Rob nor I may have had the ability at the time to help them, but we should have run to a counselor and locked in for regular sessions for the next several years. We didn't have the wisdom at the time to see it. We were being pushed by the tide of everything that drives young families in this culture, all while trying to keep our boats afloat in a turbulent ocean of pain.

My eyes pooled as Hudson and his teammates whacked baseballs in front of us. "Mom," Les comforted with her arm around my back, "you *know* we love you dearly. Love is at the root of all this, you know that, right? We know you love us, and we love you."

"I know," I said. "I do, I honestly do. It just hurts that I can't go back and redo the past." I relaxed a little and then said, "How does Dad get off the hook so easily here? He had thousands of students, coached bunches of teams, knows tons of people, and was rarely home!"

"But he didn't *give his heart* to all those people," she said. "And furthermore, moms are the center of families. They hold everything together."

"I thought that when I went to NYU I was setting an example for you both, showing how women could pursue their passions and not be limited to the role of mother. Maybe I did more damage than anything else."

"No, no!" she said. "We LOVE that you did that! But sometimes we were jealous of the friendships you made there with your classmates, that's all."

I thought back to the ways in which I would eagerly talk to my daughters about the young people in my choirs at church, or about my classmates (mostly their age) at NYU. I talked with equal fervor to my young friends about my daughters, too, thinking that they would all genuinely hit it off. Now, I was seeing that their lack of excitement was due more to their lack of confidence that I cared about them with the same enthusiasm.

"Remember the reading of your musical in New York?" Les said. "I felt like you were more interested in everyone else than me that night."

How could I have been so oblivious and neglectful? I may have been in an industry where I was fighting for my right to exist. But in doing so, I had taken for granted the love of my family around me.

"By the way, Mom," Les continued, "while we're talking about all this stuff, Lauren and I have wondered why you and Dad never tell us that we're beautiful."

This one almost made me choke. "You're kidding me, right?"

"No. You guys never say it."

Rob and I both rifled through our history with them, and all we could come up with is that other people told us all the time how beautiful they were, and we were concerned that they didn't get swelled heads about it. We *thought* it, too, of course, constantly surprised that the mix of our quirky genes had produced such good-looking kids. But apparently those thoughts never, or too rarely, made it out into the open air.

It was a lot to think about. I couldn't return to my manuscript for a long time. I had too much self-reflecting to do.

Weeks later, a friend of mine, Dr. Nancy Good, a trauma-informed therapist and international mediator, came to visit and stay the night. At breakfast, after Rob had left for work, she poured boiling water over fresh, roasted coffee grounds as I lamented how I felt about having failed my children, that of course they turned out fine, but I just had so many regrets. Then I told her about the image, burned in Leslie's memory, of my back turned away from them.

My words caught in my throat, and she turned to see my eyes spilling over. "Lisa, Lisa," she said, her soothing voice rising over her steaming cup. "You may have had your back to your daughters then. But now you have *all sides* to give them *because* you tended to your grief when you needed to."

Her words drew more tears. If it wasn't possible to go backward in time to heal my mistakes, how would I go forward?

One burning desire came rushing to the forefront. One of my biggest regrets, aside from everything else, was that we didn't travel much with our children. When Kelly was four years old and healthy, we took one short vacation to Niagara Falls as a family. We went away to the beach for a week with extended family every year, but we never traveled again as a family unit during the girls' teenage years except for the Disney trip, and then a week away two years after Kelly's death with Rob's parents. I know part of the reason was money. We had jobs in human services that didn't pay particularly well. And the girls were busy with their lives, and it was tough to get us all together, even if grief had not flattened us so terribly. But we should have tried.

Suddenly, I knew this is what I wanted to do—take each daughter away by herself, anywhere in the world she wanted to go. I couldn't make up for the past, but we could begin with a new foundation. There wasn't any better way I could see to spend our retirement funds.

The girls decided that what they wanted more than anything would be to go to a healing spa together, out in the desert with a firepit where we could sit and talk under the stars. "Why not save money since we both want the same thing," they said, "and just all go together? We'll make sure we each get time alone with you."

It is an idea that formed just before the Covid-19 pandemic arrived. Instead of traveling, we are now closing the gap of those years and the current social distancing from each other with conversation, Saturday night Zoom Bingo, and a daily Q&A game that we text back and forth.

I still hope we can one day make the trip to the spa. But their love and honesty have gone farther than any trip could possibly do in healing my heart.

CHAPTER TWENTY-FOUR

Will it ever get better?

Grieving is a sacred art...the backbone of all real peace.
— MARTÍN PRECHTEL

On a humid Friday in August of 2018, just a month before the 25th anniversary of Kelly's death, we stopped for fast food after a meeting with our financial planner. Rob paid at the counter while I went to the drink machine to fill our cups. Mine was half full when I heard, "Mommy? *Mommy, where are you?*" In a blinding flash, I was lost in space and time. I physically shuddered as tears sprang to my eyes. It was *her* voice.

Rob passed by me right then and saw that I was shaken. "What's wrong? *What happened?*"

I motioned for him to go find a table, and then I turned to look behind the condiments wall where the voice came from. There was a mother just sitting down with her little girl, eerily similar to Kelly's age and size. I looked at the child longingly for a moment, willing her to say more, then went to our table, trying to pull myself back to the present.

"That little girl over there," I explained to Rob, wiping my face with a napkin, "I heard her cry *Mommy,* and it was exactly Kelly's voice. For a second I forgot what year it was." I sobbed a little more. "I thought it was her, I really did."

His eyes softened and he reached to touch my hand. "Aww, Lis," he said. He was right there with me, wishing, hoping, and longing.

Our bodies have intelligent memory, our five senses always at the ready to be triggered by people and events that have deeply marked our lives. That memory is an antenna and can snatch emotionally complex patterns of love and trauma as quickly as a person grabbing a sweater before leaving the house. Suddenly you're *there* again, whipped back in time.

It's happened to me hundreds of times. Nine years after she passed, while waiting for a train in crowded Penn Station in New York, I saw a little girl that resembled her so closely, it took my breath away. She was wearing a floppy hat with a flower just like Kelly had worn, and she had blond hair and an outfit similar to one of Kelly's. I inched a little closer and drank her in like a hummingbird on a daylily, till the mother caught me staring and put her hand on her daughter's shoulder to steer her away from me.

We've tried to mentally age Kelly alongside her peers, imagining what she'd be like as a fourth-grader, a sixth-grader, a middle-schooler, a 33-year-old, then collapsing in sadness that they were moving along, and she wasn't.

Author Elizabeth Gilbert said, "How do you survive a tsunami of grief? By being willing to experience it without resistance." And I couldn't agree more. Grief is a dancer full of kinetic energy. At first it is the stranger who shows up at the most devastatingly inconvenient time, who hands you a dance card with its name written in every slot, when all you'd rather do is curl up in a fetal position or die. It pulls you up with strong arms and out onto the floor, presses you like a rag doll to its sides, sways, swirls, and bends you back so far that you think you'll never be able to right yourself again. Grief feels like an uninvited and unwelcome partner at first, completely out of sync with your step. All you want is for the turbulence to be *over*.

But something changes over time in the intervals of rest between all the rough movement. You look it in the eye and see something akin to the gaze of a dear friend you enjoy spending time with. You realize it wasn't willfully trying to spin you off balance in the beginning, but rather *working to stabilize you* in the trauma.

Eventually, when called out onto the floor now, you go more willingly. Your legs have become stronger, your arms more trusting of its hold, your resistance not as fierce. You still cry occasionally, but it's more softly now, not in such raw, heaving jags. You lean your head against grief's chest, feeling its warmth as you move to its music, and you begin to enjoy being led.

Grief is a friend, a companion, the energy of love that never dies. It reminds us that the doors of loss are never shut, and that our loved ones come and go in spirit as easily as they did in body. It reminds us that one day we will find each other again and realize, perhaps, that we were never as far apart as we once imagined.

I set out to understand *how did we manage, and what have we learned?* Thanks to exceptional friends, a supportive family, and a loving community, we stayed afloat. But I won't go so far as to say we managed particularly well, or made all the right choices for ourselves or each other. The girls were clearly left to deal with their grief on their own. Rob and I were shells of our normal selves. We overspent energy at our jobs and served leftovers to ourselves and our daughters.

It is tribute to the unacknowledged structures of human living, the unheralded routine of the day, the ordinary moments that no one remembers, that sustain us in ways we can take no credit for. There were the prayers that went up on our behalf from people's lips when they thought of us, and quiet acts of service that we never knew about. The intricate network of the Spirit, both seen and unseen, and the energetic love of humankind is impossible for us to comprehend or fully appreciate.

The Bible says that the Spirit intercedes for us *through wordless groans.* Sometimes I think deeply about that sound and try to imagine it. I wonder if it is similar to my own cry of grief—a yearning so core to the soul, as deep and hollowed out as the Grand Canyon, so out of its mind with love. If the Spirit intercedes like this for God's grieving, suffering, disoriented children, then we can trust that we are sustained in supernatural ways that defy our recognition and imagination.

Like a child asleep in the back seat of a car after a long day, who wakes up the next morning with no memory of having been carried to bed by their parent, *it was never up to us* to carry ourselves or manage. It was God's work all along, for both us and our children. And it's taken me all these years to fully realize this.

I'm finally learning that the initial pulling apart, though we lived in close proximity to one another, has given way to more intimacy, even with miles between us. The same has been true for our relationship with Kelly. In the beginning it felt like we were losing her. Now she resides more easily and securely within us.

I have dreamed about her as a baby, as a toddler with hair, and as a cancer patient with only fuzz for hair. My dreams were not in chronological order. She'd be a baby, then a five-year-old, then a toddler. But I have noticed that, early on, she was usually facing away from me, ignoring me, disappearing from view or slipping out of my grasp. I'd have her on my lap, feel the softness of her hair under my chin, or she'd enter the scene and then leave or not look at me. I'd wake up wrenched. All of the dreams had sad departures.

And then, maybe 18 or 20 years down the road, I had the Dream of All Dreams:

I was in Kelly's kindergarten class, and the teacher told the children it was time to lie down in their beds for naptime. I went over to Kelly's bed to tuck her in—her cancer buddy Chris was in the cot next to hers—and while never before had I made eye contact with her in a dream, this time she gently cradled my face in her hands, looked me deep in the eye and said, "Mommy, don't ever forget that I will always, *always* love you."

She lingered on my face for a long moment, smiling with the countenance of an angel. And then I woke up with tears streaming down my cheeks. But these were a different kind of tears, and this time she wasn't going away. She was reassuring me.

What toll did all this truly take? Undoubtedly the toll was horrendous for each of us, and some of that, at least for me, has been physical. Twenty-four years after Kelly's death, I consulted with a functional medicine doctor to address some personal health concerns. She scanned my paperwork and said, "You note here that these problems increased over time, but a couple times you say that you first noticed symptoms at age 40. Did something major happen then?" My eyes filled with tears, piecing together for the first time that grief had not only had a whopping emotional impact, but also a physical one.

In the crucible of sorrow, we were shaped in ways we are both aware and unaware of, and could not have been had we not gone through this. Who can put a price tag on the school of suffering? We were exposed to people and situations in an urban hospital environment that we wouldn't have encountered any other way. We were thrust out of our bleached white community into a diverse culture that enriched us and forever changed the way we want to associate with people in this life. We are more compassionate toward those who have gone through what we've been through.

Were we cheated out of the life we were supposed to have, or were we given the life we were meant to have? All I know is that we are each given a life to live, and our job is to be as creative a steward of it as we know how. We get to choose some things, and we get to resist or surrender to other things that are beyond our control.

Certainly, we were cheated out of *our agenda*. Kelly's death was a complete derailment of all our expectations for her and how we would be a family in this world. Most parents have big ideas for their children's futures. It wasn't easy feeling that carpet being pulled out from underneath us.

We will never know how different our lives may have turned out had we not gone through this. I am sure I would never have ended up at NYU, because we would've had a third child heading to college. Lauren and Leslie's tight friendship may have been different, maybe even more competitive had their sister lived to widen its dynamic. Family get-togethers may also have been even more fun, with more life variables at play, had Kelly lived to create another satellite location in our adult family. Maybe we would be less pessimistic about life, less afraid. Who can honestly know?

Barbara Brown Taylor says in her book, *An Altar in the World*, "No one longs for what he or she already has, and yet the accumulated insight of those wise about the spiritual life suggests that the reason so many of us cannot see the red X that marks the spot is because we are standing on it. The treasure we seek requires no lengthy expedition, no expensive equipment, no superior aptitude or special company. All we lack is the willingness to imagine that we already have everything we need. The only thing missing is our consent to be where we are." It's taken me years and years, but I have finally given consent to what happened to us.

Which brings me to my last question: *Was Kelly's life cut off prematurely, or did she live a full life?* How can I not now believe that Kelly lived a full life? Not the number of years we would have preferred, but the years she was given by God to live here on earth. How can I not believe Rob, Lauren, Leslie, and I have lived, and are living, the lives we're supposed to be in? How can I not give thanks for the depths of love, loss, and life that we have experienced simply by being alive and feeling everything humans do in this life? For the deeply transformative blessing that suffering has given us—as the hymn says, *how can I keep from singing?*

I can't go back and fix the sorrow and neglect of those early years when we were so splintered apart and just trying to survive. But I can take what my family has told me, and we can rewrite a new ending. Trauma that isn't transformed is trauma transferred. It either goes inward and waits, or it *moves.*

The scriptures say that there is a time to mourn, *and a time to dance.* We curl up with sorrow, but real grief cannot remain there. It has to *move.* And it doesn't know just one kind of dance; it knows a hundred different ones. It knows *you,* and it will be the loveliest, truest friend your sorrow will ever have.

Every week that I've worked on this book, I've managed to fill my trash can a third full of crumpled tissues from healing tears that let me know I am still responding to the invitation of grief. It is a dance I know well now, and a partner I doubt I will ever stop moving with.

I hope to see you out on the floor.

Acknowledgments

When I was underwater with sorrow, I'm certain I was not aware of all the people who quietly supported my family with prayers and overtures of caring. Without the support of a community, seen and unseen, none of us can survive any hardship.

There were a few whose empathy and giftedness for companioning me in the disorder and confusion of the first year were so extraordinary, that I must acknowledge them here: Rebecca Kline, Linda Metz, Sandra Smoker, Elizabeth Valle, Dawn Winey, and David Woolverton. I will never forget the loving, receptive stillness with which each of you absorbed my sorrow, and how often you freely and comfortably spoke Kelly's name. You were grief's loving attendants in the dance, wrapping my injuries with holy balm.

Carole Adkins, thank you for getting me up off the couch that first month and walking me around the neighborhood three times a week for the next three years. Steve and Doris Nolt, thank you for the two teddy bears at the bookends of Kelly's life, and for truly helpful conversations at critical points.

Bonnie Mateer and Joyce Stoltzfus, you were faithful shepherds over my heart. Linda Steele, your coordination of efforts to remember Kelly and your continued support, love, and friendship to our family is so deeply cherished.

I want to thank the Hempfield School District, namely the high school and Farmdale Elementary School—especially Kelly's teachers, Nancy Neff and Sheila Charles—for being so open to conversations about her illness and death, and for remembering our daughter in so many thoughtful and creative ways.

To those who created Kelly's Garden of the Five Senses and Kelly's Book Nook, we are profoundly grateful, even as, after 20 years, the building of the new school required that the garden be demolished. It has not destroyed your great gift in our minds.

We want to tell the volunteers who planted the Make-A-Wish dogwood in Kelly's memory in Lancaster County Central Park that while we were vaguely aware it had been planted when she died, we only discovered the 19-year-old tree for the first time—in glorious, frothy white bloom—by "accident" after we moved to the city. What a breathtaking surprise.

To Pam Landwirth, CEO of Give Kids The World, it would've been honor enough for you to tell me that you carried around my letter to your late husband, Henri, in your purse for 25 years and referenced it at this great man's memorial service. But there are no words ample enough to thank you for dedicating Kelly's Sunny Swing to our daughter's memory.

Thank you, Rennie Dyball, for your encouragement early on to proceed with this book, Sarah Chauncey, for helping me figure out the book I was really trying to write, and to those who commented on early drafts. Merle and Phyllis Good, thank you for believing in me as a writer enough to publish both of my books.

To Rila and Don Hackett, Betsy Swartz, Beth and Steve Lavender, Gregg and Susan Hurley, Laura Meyers, Candee Buckbee, Randy Riggs, and the Stephen Ministers of First Presbyterian Church, Lancaster, thank you for sharing my heart for the annual Blue Christmas service, and for lending your enormous compassion and artistic talents to create such a warm sanctuary for grieving people.

To the Bair and Huffman extended families, especially my sister, Abby Abildness, and my sisters-in-law, Linda Cullen and Ann Huffman, and to the Oberts, our dear neighbors, our story happened to all of you, too. It took me a while to comprehend just how deeply you were suffering with us.

Finally, to Rob, Lauren, and Leslie, you ground, sharpen, and inspire me every day of my life. God went all out when he gave me each of you, and then filled out our team even more with Heath, Hudson, Hadley, Holden, Ervin, Lemmy, and Bo. I couldn't love you all more.

Notes

Introductory Page

9 **necessary grief can hide:** Martín Prechtel, *The Smell of Rain on Dust: Grief and Praise* (Berkeley: North Atlantic Books, 2015), 4.

Chapter 1: Twenty-Five Septembers

15 **stages of grief:** David Kessler, "Misconceptions about the Five Stages of Grief," https://grief.com/misconceptions/.

19 **two halves make (W)hole:** choreography by Gregg Hurley, 2007.

Chapter 2: Her last day

23 **still to be lost:** Joan Didion, *Blue Nights* (New York: Alfred A. Knopf, 2011), 188.

Chapter 3: The first week

33 **stumble forward bleeding knees:** Rebecca Faber, *A Mother's Grief Observed* (Wheaton: Tyndale House Publishers, Inc., 1997), 42.

Chapter 4: The first month

42 **human soul witnessed:** Parker J. Palmer, "The Gift of Presence, The Perils of Advice," post published April 27, 2016, https://onbeing.org/blog/the-gift-of-presence-the-perils-of-advice/.

47 **very complex math problem:** Cristina Chipriano, LCSW, Director of Spanish Programs and Outreach at Bo's Place, as heard in *Speaking Grief: The Documentary* (The Pennsylvania State University, 2020), https://speakinggrief.org/documentary, 39:34.

Chapter 5: Our changing family

50 **tragedy like death of child:** Dwight D. Eisenhower, as quoted by Governor Pataki in "2004: If Tears Could Bring You Back," Sara Lukinson, *September Morning: Ten Years of Poems and Readings from the 9/11 Ceremonies* (New York: Simon & Schuster, 2012).

50 **greatest disaster of my life:** Geoffrey Perret, Eisenhower (Holbrook: Adams Media Corporation by arrangement with Random House, Inc., 1999), p.78.

52 **liken grief to amputation:** Ted Rynearson, as heard in *Speaking Grief: The Documentary* (The Pennsylvania State University, 2020), https://speakinggrief.org/documentary, 15:55.

Chapter 6: Grief on the move

57 **to fight it is to hurt yourself:** Elizabeth Gilbert, "The TED Interview," interview by Chris Anderson, October 19, 2018, https://podcasts.apple.com/us/podcast/elizabeth-gilbert-shows-up-for-everything/id1437306870?i=1000421929243&mt=2, 45:14.

62 **saying nothing is a terrible thing:** Megan Devine, as heard in *Speaking Grief: The Documentary* (The Pennsylvania State University, 2020), https://speakinggrief.org/documentary, 24:45.

65 **"Philadelphia":** Directed by Jonathan Demme, performances by Tom Hanks, Denzel Washington, Jason Robards, Mary Steenburgen, and Antonio Banderas, TriStar Pictures, 1993.

Chapter 7: Numbing the feelings

67 **kill your sadness:** S. Gluck (2013, January 29). Depression Quotes & Sayings That Capture Life with Depression, HealthyPlace. Retrieved on December 11, 2020, from https://www.healthyplace.com/insight/quotes/depression-quotes-and-sayings-about-depression.

67, 68 **rip currents:** "Rip Currents: Currents Tutorial," National Ocean Service, National Oceanic and Atmospheric Administration, U.S.Department of Commerce. https://oceanservice.noaa.gov/education/tutorial_currents/03coastal3.html.

68 **Jesus asleep in the boat:** Luke 8:22-25, Scripture taken from the Holy Bible, New International Version, NIV. Copyright © 1973, 1978, 1984, 2011 by Biblica, Inc. Used by permission of Zondervan.

Chapter 8: House of memories

75 **indescribable journey of survival:** Anonymous, retrieved on December 11, 2020 from https://www.facebook.com/MacksGlass/photos/the-loss-of-a-child-is-not-an-event-it-is-an-indescribable-journey-of-survival-t/1087702568087438/.

Chapter 9: The body's calendar

82 **memories touchstone:** Haruki Murakami, *Kafka on the Shore* (New York: Vintage Books, 2005), 98.

Chapter 10: Letting your heart catch up

89 **creativity essential response:** Henry M. Seiden, Ph.D. Specific source unknown.

Chapter 11: Making sense of a God who rips your heart out

97 **betrayal, disappointment:** Philip Yancey, *Disappointment with God: Three Questions No One Asks Aloud* (Grand Rapids: Zondervan, 1992), 263.

97 **daughter's in a better place:** "A Crisis of Faith and Octopus Aliens." *Young Sheldon.* CBS, Los Angeles. Oct. 4, 2018. Television.

100 **Covenant Prayer in the Wesleyan Tradition:** *The United Methodist Hymnal, Book of United Methodist Worship,* (King of Prussia: The United Methodist Publishing House, 1989), #607.

103 **little girl get up:** Mark 5:35-43, NIV, op. cit.

105 **pathway of lament:** Michael Card, *A Sacred Sorrow: Reaching Out to God in the Lost Language of Lament* (Colorado Springs: NavPress in alliance with Tyndale House Publishers, Inc., 2005), 19-20, 31.

107, 108 **danger of ceasing to believe in God:** N.W. Clerk (C.S. Lewis) *A Grief Observed* (United Kingdom: Faber and Faber Limited Seabury Press, 1963), 5.

109 **clots of dirt in rage:** Robert Barron with John L. Allen, Jr., *To Light a Fire on the Earth: Proclaiming the Gospel in a Secular Age* (New York: Image, 2017), 144.

109, 110 **his compassions never fail:** Lamentations 3:21-22, NIV, op. cit.

Chapter 12: When God enters our pain

113 **God is for you and with you:** Timothy Keller, *Walking with God Through Pain and Suffering* (New York: Riverhead Books, 2013), 58.

118 **fine clothes kings' palaces:** Matthew 11:7-8, NIV, op. cit.

119 **let your light shine:** Matthew 5:13-16, NIV, op. cit.

122, 123 **loveliest and saddest landscape:** Antoine de Saint-Exupéry, *The Little Prince* (Orlando: Harcourt, Inc., 1943; renewed Consuelo de Saint-Exupéry, 1971; English translation copyright, 2000 by Richard Howard), 85.

Chapter 13: Grieving alone, grieving together

124 **you cry, I cry:** Nicholas Sparks, *The Notebook* (New York: Warner Books, Inc., 1996), 166.

128 **polarize existing factors:** Jean Galica, M.A., LMFT, "The Effects of the Death of a Child on a Marriage," https://www.theravive.com/research/the-effects-of-the-death-of-a-child-on-a-marriage

128, 129 **five children in a sled:** "Interview with an Angel." *Touched by an Angel*. CBS, Los Angeles. Sept. 23, 1995. Television.

Chapter 14: The third and fourth years

132 **seed completely undone:** Cynthia Occelli, " Life podcast #44, "Chaos Precedes Transformation," https://www.cynthiaoccelli.com/life-044-chaos-precedes-transformation/, 12:38.

132 **"I Miss You Most at Christmastime":** Craig Courtney (Columbus: Beckenhorst Press, 1995), beckenhorstpress.com.

Chapter 15: Breathing again

139 **comfort in my suffering:** Psalm 119:50, NIV, op. cit.

Chapter 16: Grand jeté

146 **wild lament into dancing:** Psalm 30:11, Scripture taken from *The Message*. Copyright © 1993, 1994, 1995, 1996, 2000, 2001, 2002. Used by permission of NavPress Publishing Group.

155 **one pile of dwindling cheese:** Spencer Johnson, M.D., *Who Moved My Cheese?* (New York: G.P. Putnam's Sons Publishers, 1998, 2002).

Chapter 17: Discernment

156 **defer all decisions:** David Teems, *To Love Is Christ: 365 Devotions* (Nashville: Elm Hill Books, 2004), 19.

158, 159 **clearness committee:** Gordon T. Smith, *Listening to God in Times of Choice: The Art of Discerning God's Will* (Downers Grove: InterVarsity Press, 1997), 82.

160 **"Music of the Heart":** Miramax Films, 1999.

Chapter 18: You don't know which way the wind blows

168 **loss like a wind:** Val Uchendu, actor and writer, host of Loss to Profound, www.lostandprofoundtv.org. Specific source unknown.

171 **song, Civil War:** "Sarah," from the musical, *The Civil War*. Lyrics by Jack Murphy, Music by Frank Wildhorn, book by Gregory Boyd and Frank Wildhorn. Broadway premiere, April 22, 1999.

Chapter 19: The silent member of the family

181 **having a good dog:** Anne Lamott, posted on Twitter, December 20, 2016.

181 **dogs' sense of smell:** Alexandra Horowitz, "Inside of a Dog," as quoted in "Dogs' Dazzling Sense of Smell" by Peter Tyson on NOVA. https://www.pbs.org/wgbh/nova/article/dogs-sense-of-smell/.

Chapter 20: Grief and praise

189 **life's bigger picture from stars:** Prechtel, op. cit., 6.

Chapter 21: More people on our team

197 **knees hit the floor:** Marianne Williamson, Facebook post, August 31, 2013.

Chapter 22: Finding meaning

205 **grief lasting companion:** George Eliot, *Middlemarch* (London: Penguin Books, 1871-2, 1994), 787.

Chapter 23: My daughters reflect

211 **heart beating outside:** Mary Margaret, "Kate Beckinsale: 'Being A Mother Has Made Me Emotionally Raw'" (www.parade.com, August 2, 2012).

Chapter 24: Will it ever get better?

222 **backbone of real peace:** Prechtel, op. cit., 4.

224 **tsunami of grief:** Elizabeth Gilbert, Instagram post, June 6, 2018.

225 **wordless groans:** Romans 8:26, NIV, op. cit.

229 **X marks the spot:** Barbara Brown Taylor, *An Altar in the World* (New York: HarperCollins Publishers, 2009), xvii.

230 **time to dance:** Ecclesiastes 3:4, NIV, op. cit.

Also From
Walnut Street Books

COUSINS:
Connected through slavery, a Black woman and a White woman discover their past—and each other.

by Betty Kilby Baldwin and Phoebe Kilby

What happens when a White woman, Phoebe, contacts a Black woman, Betty, saying she suspects they are connected through slavery?

Betty finds an activist partner in Phoebe. Cousins indeed, they commit to a path of reconciliation.

Piercingly honest. Includes a working reparations project which the two women conceived together. **$14.99**

5-Ingredient Natural Recipes

by *New York Times* bestselling author, Phyllis Good (creator of the *Fix-It and Forget-It* series)

Phyllis Good's cookbooks have sold more than 14 million copies, making her one of the bestselling cookbook authors in the U.S.

A hit on QVC and elsewhere!
$19.99

For more information, go to: **www.walnutstreetbooks.com**
These books are available wherever books are sold.

About the Author

Alisa Bair is a composer and author. Her words and music have been published and performed internationally. Her previous book was *A Table for Two: A Mother and Her Young Daughter Face Death Together*.

If you would like to invite Alisa Bair to speak at an event or to a group, contact her at <u>alisabairmusic.com</u>